Class Composition & the Social Reproduction of Cultural Labor

Stevphen Shukaitis & Joanna Figiel

<.:.Min0r.:.>
.c0mp0siti0ns.

*The Wages of Dreamwork. Class Composition &
the Social Reproduction of Cultural Labor*
Stevphen Shukaitis & Joanna Figiel

ISBN 978-1-57027-407-7

Cover design by Haduhi Szukis
Interior design by Casandra Johns

Released by Minor Compositions 2024
Colchester / New York / Port Watson

Minor Compositions is a series of interventions &
provocations drawing from autonomous politics, avant-garde
aesthetics, and the revolutions of everyday life.

Minor Compositions is an imprint of Autonomedia
www.minorcompositions.info | minorcompositions@gmail.com

Distributed by Autonomedia
PO Box 568 Williamsburgh Station
Brooklyn, NY 11211

www.autonomedia.org
info@autonomedia.org

Contents

Work, What Is It Good For?............. 4

Art, Politics, and Labor................. 14

Metropolitan Strategies,
Psychogeographic Investigations 45

The Factory of Individuation 81

Knows No Weekend 119

Watermelon Politics and the Mutating
Forms of Institutional Critique Today... 164

Class Composition and the
(Non)Emergence of the Multitude 185

Non-Conclusion: To Build
Your House on the Sea 210

References 219

Acknowledgments

This book, like all books, developed over some time out of many conversations and debates that have shaped it. We are thankful to everyone involved in those exchanges – without them, the book would have been even worse. Special thanks to the folks who organized or otherwise made them possible, in particular Ryan Kopaitich and Jamie van der Klaauw from the Desire & Capital working group in Rotterdam, Mikkel Bolt Rasmussen, Geoff Cox, Joasia Krysa, the Precarious Workers Brigade, the Carrotworkers' Collective, everyone at Auto Italia, Miran Mohar, and Ned Rossiter. Thanks also to all the comrades whose presence is here even if it not always obvious, including Peter Bloom, Jack Bratich, Nin Chan, Gerald Raunig, Stefano Harney, Fred Moten, and Marina Vishmidt.

This book is dedicated to David Graeber, or to use the completely unwieldy 'action name' bestowed upon him by Genevieve at the

Festival del Pueblo in Boston in May 2002, Tikki Tikki Tembo-no Sa Rembo-chari Bari Ruchi-pip Peri Pembo...

Dreams, expectations, needs, desires... all this is labor, all this is put to work for the precarious worker. – Franco Berardi[1]

It is now clear that the autonomy and freedom the entrepreneurial initiative was supposed to bring to 'work' instead mean a much greater dependency... Modern-day capitalism find the surplus less in knowledge than in the subjective implication to which the 'immaterial worker' must yield in the same way as migrant and factory workers, users of social services, and consumers, all of whom provide an enormous quantity of free labor. – Maurizio Lazzarato[2]

Work consists of a series of such stages at deeper and deeper levels. – Sigmund Freud[3]

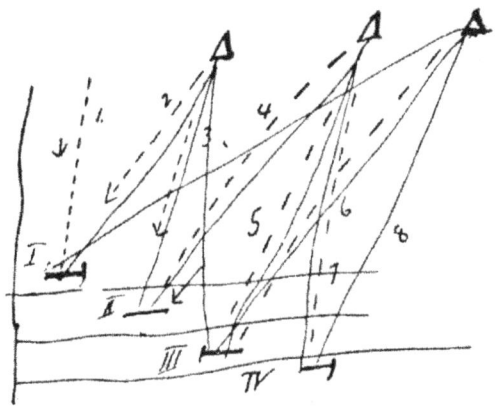

Work, What Is It Good For?

Good God Y'all...

This is a diagrammatic moment, where both Edwin Starr and autonomist theory want to bellow back, in response to that question, "Absolutely nothing!"

Indeed, there is much to be said, and it is not said nearly often enough, about the importance of practices of refusing and attempting to escape work's clutches over vast parts of our lives. And this is especially the case for when many forms of work have become all the more precarious, exploitative, and poorly paid. It's those realities that makes that reply, the desire to negate work, so satisfying. But beyond that immediate reaction, the truth is, if it were a relationship status to be posted on social media, a more honest answer would be that, well, it's complicated.

That's because when we celebrate the refusal and escape from work, it's not simply to do nothing, but often to have more time to do other things. It's to have more time for creating art and poetry, for spending time with friends and loved ones. It's really a call for an expansion of what in the classic labor slogan about the working day is described as '8 hours for what we will.' What would we do if our time was entirely within in our control, rather than constrained by the demands of work and the workplace?

Let's say that through some miracle William Benbow's call for a "Grand National Holiday," i.e., basically a month-long general strike, were achieved?[4] Granted, many people would want to take a well-earned break and rest. But soon after, many folks would turn to all those things, whether art and creative pursuits, or developing other skills, that they've long wanted to but have not been able to do. If only they had the time, they would tell themselves, forever putting them off.

A good image to succinctly summarize this fittingly is one used on the cover of this book. It's from an old magazine that was found randomly in a store in New York, and which got saved only to be hung in a university office for years, with the thought that it would be used some day, for something. It depicts a young boy who is totally engrossed in carving a wooden boat of some kind. The foreground is detailed and fleshed-out, with more developed shading and detail, from his eye focusing on the project to tools sitting nearby. By contrast, everything in the middle and background is much less completed, though we can see what appears to be a stridently indifferent chicken as well as some incompletely drawn youth, as well as a kind of mother figure who appears concerned by something, though it's not clear what.

> He worked all day on that boat, which was going to go by itself. Not steadily, of course. Some other small boy would coax him away; his mother would call him for meals, to be washed. But each time, after each interruption, he returned passionately to his boat.

The key phrase is at the end – returning passionately to the boat. This is what this book is about: the activities we pursue because they are personally gratifying and rewarding, practices we want to pursue and develop, regardless of whether they are paid or not. The focus here is particularly on those forms of creative activity and practices, creative labor if you will, and how our relationship to them changes as they are experienced as work.[5]

This is why the reply that work is good for nothing, is not, in the end, completely satisfying. Yes, many of us want to escape from the realities of work in its current forms. But that is not the same as wanting to exit from all activities that could be understood as work. Rather, it's a question: if the hegemonic and controlling nature of work were abolished, what boats would we want to return to making? This is also to ask to continue with this metaphor. How is our relationship to boat making transformed by it being both a part of our working day, and something we might do after our working day ends?[6]

Here we can briefly consider the efforts of David Hesmondhalgh and Sarah Baker to develop a model of good and bad work. In order to do so they work between a Marxist critique of work under capitalism and an ethical analysis of labor, using that as a "point of entry for a sociological evaluation of contemporary work"; they argue that this is important because classical Marxism has little to say about the subjective experience of labor.[7] This is perhaps somewhat less the case in autonomist political writing, but the point holds more generally. While the framing of forms of work as good or bad might seem simplistic, it has the advantage of not falling into the complications created by describing forms of work as alienated, which can lead into futile debates about whether this is essentialist. This is even more the case when it comes to analyzing forms of creative labor that are very engaging and rewarding, but exist in a way that they can be more exploited precisely because of how rewarding they can be for the people doing them despite poor pay or an uncertain future.

Thus, the question of what is work good for is not one that can be answered by looking at the work itself in isolation, but rather the broader social milieu that it is a part of, and takes part in reproducing. What do these varied forms of creative and cultural work produce? In this book, we start from the idea that there is a widely-shared desire to be involved in forms of work that are meaningful and engaging, and that this is particularly the case with forms of creative and artistic labor. The question is what does that desire, in its usually individuated form, produce. What forms of social reproduction are involved in and enmeshed with these forms of creative and artistic labor? We want to explore and analyze the dynamic of when the 'psychic wages' of meaningful cultural work are attached to conditions of precarity and exploitation, as they often are in our present reality. In autonomist terms, this would mean exploring and analyzing the relationship between the technical and political composition of these forms of work.

The essays contained here have been written over ten years. Sometimes when the boat to be built is a text to be completed, it can take longer to finish. Nonetheless, it would still be helpful to give a brief overview of the sections of this book and how they fit together. The first section lays out a simple sketch of the relationship between art, politics, and labor, which quickly becomes more complicated. From there we consider how bringing together the history of workers' inquiry and militant research with the Situationist practices of psychogeography and the dérive might be well suited for understanding the current situation of creative labor in the metropolis. This forms the basis of the Metropolitan Factory project, which explored shifts in our relationship with creative work when it is ourselves that have become the boss that is driving us on to work faster, longer, harder, and often for what can be described diplomatically as less than ideal pay. This project is based on an attempt to draw from the history of workers' inquiry and militant research, redeploying those ideas and practices within a much different setting, i.e., within the conditions of the contemporary cultural economy, as opposed to those of the Fordist factory.

Where does it leave us when the creative practices that we find ourselves drawn to end up being the ones through which we're most drawn into dynamics of exploitation? Can we even down tools when we're at a point where our very subjectivity, creativity, and imagination are the most valuable tools we can use?

The main argument to be explored in this book can be found in the title itself, *The Wages of Dreamwork*. What is being suggested by this title? There are two different allusions being made here. The first refers to the Wages for Housework movement. Emerging from the 1970s socialist feminism, it sought to make visible and struggle over the work of social reproduction including child care, housework, and other work involved in that. The second comes from a Biblical verse, taken from Romans 6:23, which contains the line "the wages of sin is death." What is the connection here? The working hypothesis of this overlap is not any kind of religious ideal, but rather means to propose that *the wages of dreamwork is the death of the social.* That is to say that when we enter conditions where we are looking solely, or primarily, to work for meaning and fulfillment, it ends up being through that we encounter the death of sociality. We enter a condition where we are so focused on our own creative practices that it becomes impossible to effectively discuss collective conditions, let along struggle to overcome and change them.

This is framed in quite an insightful way by Stefan Germer when he declares that belief in the power of creativity is both utopian and reactionary. How so? This is because it "gives back to the individual his labor power, and thus opposes the division of labor characteristic of capitalist societies." At the same time it is reactionary, because it "makes this reappropriation appear as an act of individual volition, independent of all social preconditions."[8] But the problem is that this is simply not true, it just doesn't work that way. Continuing within this kind of framing ends up reinforcing the idea that the struggle over pursuing one's creative practice is always an individual struggle. That is the death of the social. It is not, or at the very least shouldn't be. What we hope to do in this book is to explore and analyze the conditions of how contemporary artistic and cultural workers ended up thinking about their practices in this way, and what we might do to escape this condition, perhaps on a boat we construct together.

Notes

1   Berardi, Franco (2012) "The General Intellect is Looking for a Body," *Work, Work, Work: A Reader on Art and Labour.* Berlin: Sternberg Press, 93.

2   Lazzarato, Maurizio (2014) *Signs & Symbols: Capitalism and the Reproduction of Subjectivity.* Los Angeles: Semiotext(e), 53-54.

3   Quoted in *The Complete Letters of Sigmund Freud to Wilhelm Fliess, 1887-1904.* (1986) Ed. Jeffrey Masson. Cambridge: Harvard University Press, 247.

4   Benbow, William (n.d. [1832]). *Grand national holiday, and the congress of productive classes.* London: Pelagian.

5   Throughout this book when, like Allen Iverson, we're talking about practice, we mean it not just as something people do, but in the fuller sense developed by Alisdair MacIntyre, as a coherent and complex form of cooperative human activity "through which goods internal to that form of activity are realized in the course of trying to achieve those standards of excellence which are appropriate to, and partially definitive of, that form of activity, with the result that human powers to achieve excellence, and human conceptions of the ends and goods involved, are systematically extended." MacIntyre, Alastair (1984) *After Virtue: A Study in Moral Theory.* Notre Dame: Notre Dame University Press, 187.

6   On this see Ranciere, Jacques (1989) *The Nights of Labor: The Workers' Dream in Nineteenth Century France.* Philadelphia: Temple University Press.

7   Hesmondhalgh, David and Sarah Baker (2010) *Creative Labour: Media Work in Three Cultural Industries.* New York: Routledge, 25/27.

8   Germer, Stefan, (2007) "Beuys, Haacke, Broodthaers," *Joseph Beuys: The Reader.* Claudia Mesch and Viola Michely. Cambridge: MIT Press, 58.

Art, Politics, and Labor

> In the period following World War II, artists came to see themselves not as artists producing (in) a dreamworld but as workers in capitalist America. They navigated the avant-garde desire to merge art and life under dramatically different social structures than their Modernist predecessors. – Helen Molesworth[1]

Art, politics, and labor: where are we to begin? Given the amazing degree of variation in understanding each of the areas, trying to pin down how they relate to each other and overlap could easily result in a vast array of possible approaches starting from different conceptions. Taking just two of these areas leads one into vast academic literatures. Given the near impossibility of providing a comprehensive account, this chapter will take a more thematic approach, gesturing to key areas of concern to be explored. As a starting point, we can consider three figures illustrating the relationship between art, labor, and politics in interesting ways, some more celebrated as paradigmatic figures of art history than others.

First, let us consider Marcel Duchamp. While mentioning Duchamp is almost required in many contexts, he is fascinating as a figure precisely for the way he helped to redefine all three areas above. From his involvement with the Dadaists, which is still drawn from heavily in thinking about the politics of art, to transforming what could be understood as art practice itself through the idea of the readymade. In many ways Duchamp can be understood as the avant-garde figure whose shock of the new serves to disrupt and redefine established methods of artistic production, relationship to politics and the functioning of markets.[2]

Secondly, we could consider Yves Klein, whose all too short career in Paris in the mid-20th century is impressive for how quickly it developed. Klein cultivated a well-thought-out artistic celebrity image, and likewise maintained links with avant-garde currents of the time. He managed to turn disruptive gestures, from the exhibition of monochromatic paintings to galleries apparently empty of all content, and the trademarking of his own shade of blue, into both artistic credibility and financial success. In some of his most interesting pieces he would engage in the sale of an artwork possessing no apparent visible existence in the world, what he would call "zones of immaterial pictorial sensibility," which he would exchange only for pure gold.[3] Similarly to Duchamp, his practices can be seen to redefine the nature of artistic practice, how value is produced by art, and the politics involved.

Finally, we could turn to Gustav Metzger, who as part of the UK art scene in the 1960s developed the idea and practice of autodestructive, as well as autocreative, art. Metzger spent years elaborating a sense of politics based around the power of art institutions and the importance of ecological thinking. He proposed the years 1977-1980 as "years without art" thus helping to develop what has been called since then the idea of the "art strike." The art strike, along with its more recent iterations, has been taken up as a form of labor struggle and politics designed to disrupt the gallery system and question the role of the artist and the place of the arts within the cultural economy.[4]

These are three figures, moments, or conjunctions of art, politics, and labor. Needless to say, there are many more. Starting from here, we could frame them in an admittedly crude but hopefully useful model for showing how they relate. This can be done by evaluating particular artists or artistic movements and practices based on their relationship to the market, and whether they tend to emphasize an individual or collective orientation. Does the artist or movement exhibit an articulated attitude or relationship to the labor (as well as commodification) – does it embrace or celebrate it? Or an attitude that is quite critical of the market, perhaps espousing an anti-capitalist stance or elaborating a different notion of value and social organization? Similarly, for the question of orientation, is it primarily around the notion of individual creation or form of social or collective creation? In this first attempt to frame the relationship between art, markets, and politics we could thus understand artistic politics as formed through how arts and markets relate to each other, in variations of embrace and celebration, to attempts to negate or work around them or do away with them altogether.

Most typically when we think of art and artists there is a tendency to fall back on an assumption of individual artists, the celebration of the artist as the individual genius, the creator of something new out of nothing. This kind of assumption is what leads to any number of news stories about, for instance, the recent sale of some piece by a dead 'master' for an exorbitant sum of money.[5] The celebration of the artist as the individual genius is embedded in a larger set of assumptions about what counts as valuable within the arts and the art world, and how this value is produced.[6] Likewise, this is also connected to the positions of critics and their associated modes of valuing, both in monetary and symbolic terms, of works of art. Roger Taylor has argued that the ethos of the 'individual genius' who possesses a pre-ordained creativity or talent blocks off others engaging in artistic activity from seeing themselves as workers.[7] The politics of connecting arts and labor here is found only in enabling the recognition of certain forms of activity as valid, as being art, or in terms of how they are valued. This can be seen to operate through the way that people who work within the arts and creative sectors would not identify themselves, or be identified, as artists. They do not seem themselves as 'mere' workers, yet their work is not regarded on the same pane as the work of 'the artist.'

The art world is happy to celebrate the work of the individual artist who is quite critical of capitalism, the state, and the operations of power. In many cases it may actually appreciate the commercial value of certain political approaches, concepts, or understandings precisely because of how they can generate further interest (and sales) in the artist in question. This seems to especially be the case in recent times when the value and social visibility of interventionist art, political art, has increased greatly. As has been wryly noted before, there is perhaps nothing as commercial as the anti-commercial artists. In these cases 'politics' becomes the content of a work that can be celebrated, rather than something that is enacted in its form, or the relations involved in the process of artistic production itself, or the kinds of labor that are involved. This is why, for instance, the art world has been more than content to conduct and facilitate endless discussions about precarity, creativity, and the arts – all the while reproducing the very conditions of precarious work and life in terms of funding, labor practices and arrangements, while engaging in these discussions. Addressing precarity happens at the level of content, rather than by changing the conditions of the art world where the discussion occurs.[8]

Nearly diametrically opposed to this are collectively oriented artistic practices openly rebuking market relations. This is where most avant-garde movements, from Constructivism to Surrealism, or those who participated in art strikes, would be located. There is a tendency for artistic work that falls into this category to be respected less on the grounds that it is not good art, that it is propaganda, and thus does not need to be taken very seriously. Or, much of it is simply dismissed as "not art at all." As Lucy Lippard commented, the art world prefers "museum quality resistance" rather than forms that become too engaged: "art that is too specific, that names, about politics, or place, or anything else, is not marketable until it is abstracted, generalized, defused."[9] Collectively oriented practices that are not market-oriented tend to be shaped around enunciating different kinds of value other than market ones, for instance in the Constructivist practice of attempting to build a socialist society through art, or the Surrealist exploration of the collective unconscious. Here we could include artistic practices that are designed to reproduce other forms of social relationships, such as through the idea of artistic citizenship, or propping up religious authority.[10] This could also include collectivist activist practices that remain on the fringes of the art world, possibly exploiting the ambiguity of being inside/outside the art world, but which are then read and/or classified as art.

In recent years, a number of groups in Europe and in the US are organizing around the questions of art, labor, and value. In the UK, the Precarious Workers Brigade emerged from the Carrotworkers Collective that previously worked specifically around the increasing reliance on exploitation of interns and unpaid workers within the art world. Today, PWB have expanded to deal with wider issues of precarious conditions of working and living within in the arts and cultural, as well as education sector and beyond. Working between London, Berlin, New York and Bucharest, Artleaks is a collective platform of artists and curators, focusing on exposing (and naming and shaming) labor exploitation, slander, intimidation, and blackmail occurring within the art world. US-based WAGE, Working Artists in the Greater Economy, ran a survey about the economic experiences of visual and performing artists who worked with non-profit arts organizations and museums, finding that "58% of artists who exhibited at a New York non-profit organization between 2005 and 2010 received no form of payment, compensation, or reimbursement – including the coverage of any expenses." In Denmark, UKK (Unge Kunstnere og Kunstformidlere, or 'Young artists and art workers') have presented a broad survey of working conditions of their members. A more informal group Haben und Brauchen, formed to further discussions about working conditions of artists and cultural producers, as well as the conditions of production and valuation of art and culture, in a city that prides itself on both thriving art scene and large numbers of cultural producers, Berlin.[11]

Lastly, we could look at practices that are collectively oriented and pro-market. These are comparatively rarer, but could include figures such as Theaster Gates who are unambiguous in their embrace of the market, but embrace it in order to create other kinds of social relationships.[12] Gates has been quite explicit about his approach of turning art into capital through sales, and then using that capital to acquire property for community development efforts and projects, which then form the social basis for the creation of new art projects. Conceptually, this proceeds in a virtuous circle of expansion. Here we could also include the history of artists' cooperatives, or the formation of cooperatives within Fluxus.[13] Oftentimes here, the acceptance of market relations is one of a pragmatic nature, rather than an ideological decision. Although the same could be argued similarly for forms of art practice rejecting market relations: at times that could be a pragmatic decision.

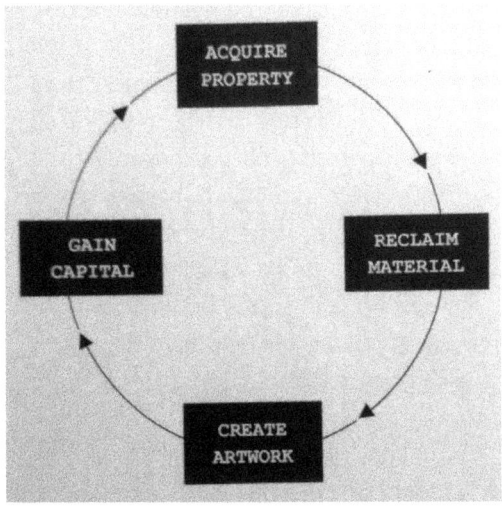

Seven Days in What?

> the pervasive decommodification of cultural labor today may be interpreted as one response to what various critics have understood as the late-twentieth-century shifting composition of value, whether that moment is diagnosed as the end of the Keynesian compact, or the rise of financialization, or the neoliberalization of the state…In art, decommodified labor reveals that the tautological time of real subsumption has been captured and transformed within the space of the aesthetic. Decommodified labor appears as a strange pause in accumulative temporality. It was always the possibility of nonwork that conceptually sustained not only the autonomy of art but also the category of the aesthetic itself. – Leigh Claire La Berge, *Wages Against Artwork*[14]

In laying out this model of framing the relationship between politics, art and the labor there is an immediate problem. It is the very concern we began with, namely that a model like this is far too simple. These positions are hard to nail down with this degree of clarity, and change over time. For instance, we could look at the ways that collectively oriented anti-market practices generate interest and social value, which are then rendered by artists into personal fame and economic success. This could be called the Boltanski and Chiapello effect for the way they describe how artistic critiques of the market have been absorbed into forming a "new spirit of capitalism" for the present.[15]

More importantly, it is clearly the case that the art world, the market, and politics are not one, monolithic thing. Thus, the way that art, politics, and markets are related varies immensely by the particular subsection and any part of them we are discussing. The way in which value is produced there, and the kinds of value that are produced in an overall sense, can only be found within the details. In other words, the politics possible within a commercial gallery space would vary quite significantly from those of street art, or the art school, even if these spaces at times cross over each other. Here we could consider the descriptions provided by Sarah Thornton in *Seven Days in the Art World*.[16] While it is true that Thornton tends to only focus on the shiny and glitzy aspects of the art world, her description and categorization of the worlds of experience found there is quite useful. Although Thornton tends to omit those in lower rank positions, her book does include accounts of the work of studio and gallery assistants. Still, the chapters that mention the low-paid art workers are centered on the glamour and the glitz of the situations they describe, and fail to include any interviews or insights into the actual daily work processes, politics, and organization of work. Thornton divides the art world into the space of the auction, the art school crit session, the art fair, prizes and prize giving, art magazine production, the studio space, and the biennale. By breaking the art world down into multiple spaces, she demonstrates that it is not a monolith, and that each particular area is engaged in a different form of value production and is animated by varying forms of social relationships.

As Thornton herself suggests, the art world is not a system or a smooth functioning machine, but is better understood as a "conflicted cluster of subcultures – each of which embrace different definitions of art."[17] Each sector could thus be understood to contain a different relationship between art, politics, and markets in that it creates different forms of value by its activity. So when Thornton notes that a Turner Prize nomination increases the selling price for works by an artist by one third, and that winning doubles the price, this is a clear indication of how value is produced in that act of prize giving, and thus the politics of articulating a relationship between art and the market.[18] This quickly multiplies the relationship and spaces for co-articulating the relationship between politics, art, and the market. We can thus understand how even for one artist, practice, or movement the politics and value associated with them is not solely found within their own actions, but in how they interact with a distributed set of interactions and roles across a whole range of spaces and institutions. Indeed, even if the focus was limited to a specific city and time, for instance in the way Fletcher and Helmreich have done with London art markets in the 19th century,[19] the social shaping of the art market and the politics of that are quite complex and varied.

Art and Value Production

> artistic productivity arises from the alliance between the artist's specific skills and the condition of coinciding with one's desire. And this is precisely the ideal formula which the neoliberal enterprise would like

to reproduce on a large scale, evidently with the provision that each employee's 'own desire' must be aligned with the desire of the enterprise. But there comes a point when hierarchical relaxation, the better to give free rein to the creativity of the 'creatives', begins to contradict the very existence of the structure of capital. – Frédéric Lordon[20]

Perhaps rather than getting caught up within the details of the relationship between politics, arts, and labor, it would be more useful to trace that relationship back to a question that connects them all, namely: how does art produce value? We could approach this question starting from something like a labor theory of culture.[21] From an understanding of this value production, we can then develop an approach to politics. There is always something difficult about directly discussing value formation, and perhaps even more so when discussing how artistic labor produces value. Questions of value production often stand in as a proxy for providing the basis for politics, lending legitimacy to certain kinds of interventions or modes of organizing in Marxist politics, or providing the prime logic for decision-making within capitalism. In this sense one can say that in the same way that labor power is more than itself, the question of value production is always more than itself, precisely because of how it connects to other concerns and realities. And this in some ways serves to explain the difficulty in approaching it, for as Diedrich Diederichsen suggests, paraphrasing Marx, "Value, therefore, does not have its description branded on its forehead; it rather transforms every product of labor into a social hieroglyphic... this hieroglyphic speaks of something, but it is impossible to tell by looking at it what it is speaking of."[22]

The question that concerns us here are the forms of social valuation produced by artistic practices and intervention. Or, taking up the argument of Peter Burger,[23] it would be to ask if the role of the avant-garde has been to attempt to bring art back into daily life, then what modes of interaction and value did this movement produce? In Burger's narration of the historical avant-garde this becomes a story of a rejection of traditional art institutions and formats that results in transforming the logic of the art institution and art practice more generally, as it comes to value other forms of artistic practice and production than it had before. Antagonism is converted into new forms of artistic productivity.

This is not, however, to fall back on an argument that artistic practices are merely reflections of underlying economic structures that determine them, as would likely be the case in an older style of Marxist analysis that relies on a base-superstructure model. As Jacques Attali argued in his important book *Noise*,[24] modes of artistic production can precede and can actually forecast broader changes in economic interactions. Pascal Gielen has expanded this argument with his recent work on the artistic multitude, arguing that the art world served as social laboratory for the development of the post-Fordist work ethic.[25] The purpose of examining changing modes of value and production in the art world is then not necessarily to remain in one's concerns in the art world. In fact, there is too great a tendency for discussions of art and labor to remain within the circuit of concerns of the art world exclusively, rather than considering how these interactions have become more generalized and expanded beyond the art world.

But perhaps we are yet again getting a bit ahead of ourselves, as is easy to do in such consideration. Taking a step back, we can return to what seems like it should be quite a basic question. When we speak of value being created in an artistic process, value being created by artistic labor, how exactly is that value created? There is something particularly slippery in talking about value production in artistic labor, and the slippery nature of this discussion can easily lead one back into an almost neoliberal conception of value production, one that could be held even despite the stated intentions of the person making claims about artistic labor.

What are the main models of value production and labor? For the sake of simplicity, let's say there are two main approaches, to which a third kind can be added. The first approach would be to argue that value is created through the process of exchange itself. That is to say, that value is the product of social exchange, the outward expression of valuation of whatever goods and services are discussed. Value in this sense is created within the process of exchange itself, rather than being a formal characteristic that existed before the exchange process. Perhaps the best expression of this can be found in the work of Georg Simmel and more generally in neoclassical conceptions of value production and utility developed within neoclassical economic thinking but generalized since then.[26]

Contrasted to this, one could pose a more traditionally Marxist conception of value, which is that value is the substance produced by labor power which is then valorized through circulation and accrued eventually into the further development of capital accumulation. Although this is admittedly a very crude rendering of complex debates around value production, the essential aspect for the consideration here is that value is an attribute related to labor itself, and thus value production occurs prior to an exchange happening within the marketplace. This is Marx's point about trying to understand commodity production not through an analysis of the market and its appearances, but rather in relation to the labor and value practices that happen within "the hidden abode of production."

Here we should also pause to gesture to models of value production that have extended and developed these ideas in quite fruitful directions, and in particular David Graeber's anthropological model of value production as framework for evaluating the importance of actions and modes of being that are already in motion.[27] Graeber's work in this direction is formed by the bringing together of Marxist political economy with the ideas and work of Marcel Mauss, and provides a way of thinking value in a broader sense. This has been taken up by Massimo De Angelis, who expands this into a framework of value practices and value struggles around ways of living,[28] and could be further expanded along the line that Bruno Gulli has sketched out through exploring how labor functions as a core concept for social and political ontologies.[29] Gulli proceeds from his poetic conception of labor to a politics that recuperates what political economy often forgets: culture, care, and ethics of singular becomings that are not determined by economic value.

The main reason why we bring up modes of value production is not that we want to get into a long exploration of them, but to point out that they seem to have difficulty when applied to the ways in which artistic labor produces value. Or, we could rather say, that Marxist approaches to value production come into the greatest difficulty. This can be seen when we take the clichéd scenario of any recent news article discussing how a particular work by this or that master artist has sold for some new record-breaking amount. Now, if value is produced by the labor necessary for the creation of the piece, whether that piece is a piece of steel or painting, it does not make sense to say a piece would contain more value one day, rather than the day before, particularly when the artist has been dead for decades if not centuries. In this case, it would be easy enough to take such instances as a kind of false bubble effect of capitalist market relations that bears no semblance to the substance of value contained in the work. There might be some truth to that, but there is more than just that.

The value of the labors of circulation is that which produces the social evaluation of worth or significance of whatever it is in question. For the work of the old master that is now valued in prices beyond all reasonable imagination, it is not simply that the piece itself has magically accrued value. Rather, there is a whole industry of discussing and evaluating the importance of artists and their work, displaying and exhibiting them, commenting and discussing, cataloging and curating, constructing narratives, all the work that creates what Howard Becker very accurately describes as "art worlds."[30] The labors of circulation thus are the labors that curators, commentators, galleries, art sales – in short all the figures that make the art world work, that make images and ideas circulate – take part in. This is precisely the point that Isabelle Graw makes when she describes critics as marketers, which is to say as boosters of art value, and thus participating in a form of labor that amasses symbolic value which can be converted into economic value on the market.[31] This means that it is not the case that a piece has mysteriously managed to increase in value through its own efforts – it is a mystical conception of value, art, and labor. Rather, it is the way that the diffuse labors flowing through art worlds come to attach themselves to individual pieces, or are rendered into market prices of these works.

Value and the artistic mode of production

> The social role of waged work has been so naturalized as to seem necessary and inevitable, something that might be tinkered with but never escaped... This effort to make work at once public and political is, then, one way to counter the forces that would naturalize, privatize, individualize, ontologize, and also, thereby, depoliticize it. – Kathi Weeks[32]

What is most useful in thinking about the labor of circulation and how that produces value in art work is less the importance of that dynamic specifically in the art world itself, but more what happens when such dynamic is spread beyond the boundaries of the specific artist economy and becomes a more general dynamic. Or as Chin-Tao Wu has argued in her book *Privatizing Culture*, the way that art, the business world, and politics have entered "clandestine symbiotic relationship" through which those enmeshed in the overlapping of these networks find themselves in an ideal position to transform economic capital into cultural capital and cultural capital into economic capital, all mediated through the circulatory auras of the art world.[33]

This could be described, following the work of Sharon Zukin, as the rise of an artistic mode of production, one based upon utilizing the same dynamics of circulatory labor in the remodeling of lifestyles, neighborhoods, and ways of life into a generalized mode of value production.[34] It can be recalled that Zukin's work looked at the transformation of Manhattan in the 1960s and 1970s as former industrial spaces were taken over firsts by artists who used them as combined studio and work spaces. This is the emergence of the 'loft economy' and transformation of Lower Manhattan from an industrial space into another form of value production. This is when a sign proclaiming 'artist in residence' was hung not for the purpose of advertising some fancy new program, but rather to inform the fire department that there were people living in these industrial spaces (which they would not have otherwise assumed).

The use of former industrial space for mixed use, the complete combining of living and working into an integrated mode of artistic production, becomes a key model for schemes of urban renewal and development based around the cultural cache of the arts. This ends up forming a mode of gentrification and development that is applied far beyond the context of New York, and is used to fuel property development in many other locations. In Zukin's description of this process in New York, the main victims of it were not the local residents, but the workers from the workspaces that were displaced. And so, importantly, artists end up finding themselves acting as inadvertent proxy in the gentrification process, for real estate booms and investment, with the 'Bohemian' lifestyles afforded by these spaces serving as model for imitation by the middle class. Artists also further develop modes of combining work and life that, because of it is impossible to clearly delineate them, end up serving to intensify and deepen forms of labor and attachment to work when they are generalized beyond the arts economy.

This argument has been explored by Bohm and Land by specifically looking at the ways in which notions of value are shaped within cultural policy discourse, and how they have shifted over time.[35] Bohm and Land argue that in the UK over the past fifteen years there was a shift in how value in the cultural economy is conceived: from an earlier conception that the value of the arts in their potential to generate revenue to one of forms of indirect value creation, such as generating creativity, fostering employability and social inclusion, and other such conditions. Arguably, in recent years, there has been a shift away from this indirect model of artistic value creation back to the direct production of revenue. The ongoing economic and social crises have certainly contributed to this trend, or perhaps more accurately, provided a convenient explanation for it. Regardless of the changing trends in arts and cultural policy, it is this social value of the arts and cultural labor – more generally, how they take part in renewing social bonds and sociality – that is precisely not recognized or rewarded. As Randy Martin argues, the connection created by the artwork is the work of art itself; art makes exchange possible but is not of it – and therefore paradoxically falls out of the accounting of the labors involved in maintaining the conditions, the very forms of sociability, that make possible exchange itself.[36]

An Exceptional Arts Economy? And Its Politics?

> the expression the politics of art might not even be appropriate insofar as it suggests that there is a politics inherent in art… it is more appropriate to speak of the social struggles over the politicity of aesthetic practices. – Gabriel Rockhill[37]

Finally, let us end with a brief consideration of whether the economy of the arts is in any way exceptional. This is the question asked by the economist Hans Abbing in his book *Why Are Artists Poor?*[38] His answer involves an analysis of the mixed structures of motivation, value, and outcomes that characterize the art world – how it is suspended, and torn between an economy based on gifts and social values, and market-oriented values. But the formulation of the arts as exceptional is problematic, because even if this was once the case, the expansion of the arts and cultural economy, and its structures of motivation and relationship to work, has spread far beyond the borders of the art world. The passionate and self-motivated labor of the artisan, which has long been part of explaining why artists are willing to accept less desirable working conditions and income because of the (supposedly) higher degree of meaning found in their work, has been taken up by management theory and practices within the knowledge economy and post-Fordist working practices. This does not mean that it is no longer interesting or worthwhile to analyze the politics of art markets and cultures, but rather that these dynamics have become much more important precisely because they have been generalized further beyond the art world itself.

Further, to draw from the ideas of Pierre Bourdieu and Howard Becker, we could say that the art worlds have moved from existing mainly as a form of social reproduction (taste as class structure) to a position much more directly enmeshed in production. The relationship between art, labor, and politics is thus one of a composition of forces: forms of labor, political action, and social life that are intermingled with one another. Politics is not separate from the relations of the art world, it cannot be relegated to the content of artistic production. For arts' labor politics is found in the articulation of the relationship between art and the labor, and the forms of organization and sociality that emerge and that are sustained by that very conjunction.

Notes

1. Molesworth, Helen (2003) *Work Ethic*. University Park: Pennsylvania State University Press, 26-27.
2. De Duve, Thierry (1996) *Kant After Duchamp*. Cambridge: MIT University Press.
3. Riout, Denys (2010) *Yves Klein: Expressing the Immaterial*. Paris: Editions Dilecta. See also Brougher, Kerry et al. (2010) *Yves Klein: With the Void, Full Powers*. Washington, DC: Walker Art Center.
4. Home, Stewart (1991) *The Neoist Manifestos/The Art Strike Papers*. Stirling: AK Press.
5. Findlay, Michael (2012) *The Value of Art: Money, Power, Beauty*. London: Prestel Publishing.
6. Klamer, Arjo, ed. (1996) *The Value of Culture: On the Relationship between Economics and Arts*. Amsterdam: Amsterdam University Press.
7. Taylor, Roger (1978) *Art, an Enemy of the People*. London: Harvester Press. See also Rockhill (2014).
8. Or treating precarity as something recent, as opposed to tracing back a longer history. See for instance Bologna (2018)
9. Lippard, Lucy (1973) *Six Years: The Dematerialization of the Art Object*. New York: Praeger, xxi.
10. On artistic citizenship see Schmidt and Martin (2006); on art and religious authority see Freedland (2001).
11. For more information on these groups see: Precarious Workers Brigade (http://precariousworkersbrigade.tumblr.com/); Artleaks (http://art-leaks.org); WAGE, Working Artists in the Greater Economy (www.wageforwork.com); UKK, Unge Kunstnere og Kunstformidlere, or 'Young artists and art workers' (http://www.ukk.dk); Haben und Brauchen (www.habenundbrauchen.de).
12. Gates, Theaster (2012) *Theaster Gates: 12 Ballads for Hugenot House*. Cologne: Walther Konig.

13 Readies, DJ (2012) *Intimate Bureaucracies*. Brooklyn: Punctum Books.
14 La Berge, Leigh Claire (2019) *Wages Against Artwork: Decommodified Labor and the Claims of Socially Engaged Art*. Durham: Duke University Press, 9/27.
15 Boltanski, Luc and Chiapello, Eve (2005) *The New Spirit of Capitalism*. London: Verso.
16 Thornton, Sarah (2008) *Seven Days in the Art World*. London: Granta.
17 Ibid., xix.
18 Ibid., 140.
19 Fletcher, Pamela and Anne Helmreich, Eds. (2012) *The Rise of the Modern Art Market in London, 1850-1939*. Manchester: Manchester University Press.
20 Lordon, Frédéric (2014) *Willing Slaves of Capital: Spinoza And Marx On Desire*. London: Verso, 124.
21 Woolfson, Charles (1982) *The Labour Theory of Culture*. London: Routledge & Keegan Paul.
22 Diederichsen, Diedrich (2008) *On (Surplus) Value in Art*. Berlin: Sternberg Press, 22.
23 Burger, Peter (1984) *Theory of the Avant-Garde*. Minneapolis: University of Minnesota Press.
24 Attali, Jacques (1985) *Noise: The Political Economy of Music*. Minneapolis: University of Minnesota Press.
25 Gielen, Pascal (2009) *The Murmuring of the Artistic Multitude: Global Art, Memory and Post-Fordism*. Amsterdam: Valiz.
26 Simmel, Georg (2004) *The Philosophy of Money*. New York: Routledge.
27 Graeber, David (2001) *Toward an Anthropological Theory of Value: The False Coin of Our Own Dreams*. New York: Palgrave.
28 De Angelis, Massimo (2007) *The Beginning of History: Value Struggles and Global Capital*. London: Pluto.
29 Gulli, Bruno (2005) *Labor of Fire: The Ontology of Labor Between Economy and Culture*. Philadelphia:

Temple University Press; and Gulli, Bruno (2010) *Earthly Plenitudes: A Study on Sovereignty and Labor.* Philadelphia: Temple University Press.

30 Becker, Howard (2008) *Art Worlds.* Berkley: University of California Press.

31 Graw, Isabelle (2010) *High Price: Art Between the Market and Celebrity Culture.* Berlin: Sternberg Press.

32 Weeks, Kathi (2011) *The Problem with Work: Feminism, Marxism, Antiwork Politics, and Postwork Imaginaries.* Durham: Duke University Press, 7.

33 Wu, Chin-Tao (2002) *Privatising Culture: Corporate Art Intervention Since the 1980s.* London: Verso, 120.

34 Zukin, Sharon (1989) *Loft Living: Culture and Capital in Urban Change.* New Brunswick: Rutgers University Press

35 Böhm, Steffen and Land, Chris (2009) "No Measure for Culture? Value in the New Economy," *Capital & Class* 97: 75-98.

36 Martin, Randy (1990) *Performance as Political Act: The Embodied Self.* New York: Praeger, 83.

37 Rockhill, Gabriel (2014) *Radical History and the Politics of Art.* New York: Columbia University Press, 7.

38 Abbing, Hans (2004) *Why Are Artists Poor?: The Exceptional Economy of the Arts.* Amsterdam: Amsterdam University Press. For more on the exceptionalism of the economy of the arts, see also Beech (2016).

Metropolitan Strategies, Psychogeographic Investigations

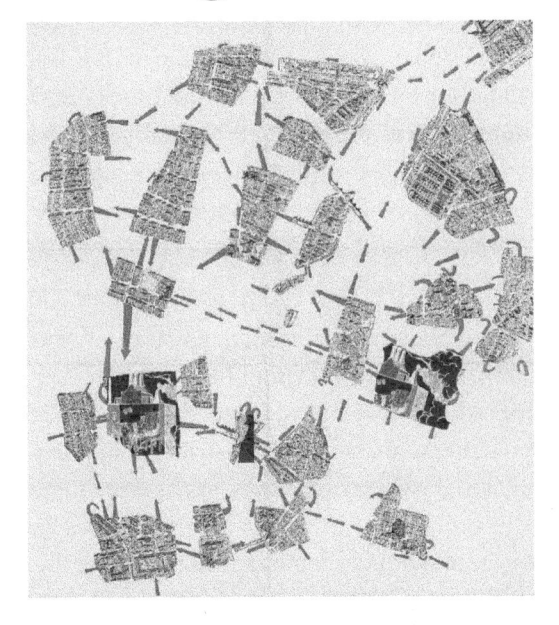

We are bored in the city... or so proclaimed Ivan Chtcheglov in his 1953 essay "Formula for a New Urbanism."[1] With this striking call, Chtcheglov set out with his other comrades and fellow travelers to explore new ways of adventuring through the city, imagining and encountering it, and from that to provoke moments of social rupture they hoped would upturn and reshape the entire social and political fabric. This adventure, initially inaugurated in the form of the Letterist International, and developing in the 1950s and 1960s into the Situationist International, sought ways to contest Fordist capitalism by fusing together the history and strategies of avant-garde arts, Marxist politics, and a focus on everyday interactions that was more ludic while not losing its sense of the necessity to continually embody and elaborate political strategies.

Meanwhile, in the Italian context of the 1960s and 1970s, a form of heretical Marxism flourished, developing from the seemingly spontaneous massive wildcat strikes of migrant industrial workers who were just as discontent with unions and left wing political parties as they were with the dehumanizing nature of the assembly line. They called not for the dignity of labor or for higher wages, but for exiting the factory and the refusal of work altogether. During the 1970s these struggles moved from the factory to the territory of the city itself, expanding from a focus on the wage / waged labor to a much broader contestation of social reproduction, housing, culture, and creativity. Far from putting forward demands of 'work for life' precarity itself was celebrated as positive and beautiful, as an escape from the drudgery of the industrial system.

Both of these strains of politics and theory continue to provide inspiration for the constant rethinking and reformulation of methods and approaches for confronting capitalism. But they also require some reworking, as the Fordist capitalism that they were contesting has changed dramatically since then. We might say that far from being bored in the city, or crying out to refuse work and exit the productive process, it is these very methods and ideas that are blocked off today in the shifting conditions of neoliberal post-Fordist capitalism.[2] The forms of play, desire, and collectivity the Situationists worked from have been rendered into new forms of capital accumulation. Imagination, creativity, and revolt itself have been put to work through the cultural industries, while sites of political antagonism are celebrated as heritage and branding for cities. Capital increasingly relies upon forms of 'free labor' and self-directed sociality that are necessary to its reproduction, even while not directly controlled by it. Likewise, many attempts to escape from work find themselves captured and rendered into new forms of laboring activity, whether through social media networks, the gathering of geolocation data, and the continual shifting of management practice that turns discontent with work into new forms of humanistic management techniques that deepen the level at which discipline operates by appearing to remedy and address the frustrations with work itself. In short, we have become what Peter Fleming and Carl Cederstrom describe as "dead men working," unable to escape from meaningless and everlasting forms of work.[3] And beyond this, we also work in our sleep, see Rob Lucas, who suggests that the only real escape from work for us now would be serious illness, our body going on strike.[4]

In many ways, this is not a new story at all. It is what Boltanski and Chiapello described as the "new spirit of capitalism," where the ideas and energies of artistic and social critique have been separated from each other and turned into devices for the reconfiguration of continued exploitation.[5] The Situationists likewise warned that half making a revolution only served to prepare one's own grave. And the autonomist tradition has as its core the notion that capital develops precisely through how it can find ways to turn moments of social antagonism into new modes of accumulation. But despite the near inevitability of some dynamic of recuperation from occurring, this still tends to leave social and political movements disoriented when it occurs, leading to a sense that what Colectivo Situaciones call "the times of impasse" has been reached.[6]

There is some truth in the stories of de-potentialization. In autonomist terms, this would be described as class decomposition. Any radical politics can only claim such a status, effectiveness, for how it intervenes in a specific social and historical situation. There is nothing inherently radical about an idea or tactic; it is rather its embedded and effects, how it is lived and elaborated, that gives it this character. Thus, it should come as no surprise that claims, ideas, and actions formulated to contest a specific mode and moment of capitalist development would not necessarily have the same importance or value within the present. But that does not mean they possess no value; rather, what is necessary is working out and reformulating them in ways that address the present conjuncture(s).

The aim of this chapter is to bring together concepts from the Situationists, such as the practice of psychogeography and unitary urbanism, with recent writings on the shaping of the metropolis today. It will also take up the autonomist concepts of class composition analysis and conducting a workers' inquiry, suggesting that it can be usefully combined with Situationist ideas about forging new tools for contesting neoliberalism. Insofar as the current configuration of neoliberal capitalism is dependent upon apparently free forms of sociality, on free labor, imagination, creativity, and upon the operations of the metropolis itself, it becomes all the more important to investigate the ongoing shaping of these activities – and to elaborate new political strategies from this approach.[7] For instance, if the metropolis were a factory, how would it go on strike? If all of everyday life and communication is put to work, how can we throw down our tools? And if capital attempts to recuperate all forms of radical politics in order to turn them into new energies for continued accumulation, is a strategy of concealment or incomprehensibility one possible way to escape these dynamics?

Lost in the city, we find ourselves

The notion of psychogeography (as well as many other ideas proposed by the Situationists) appears frequently within political and artistic discussions. Indeed, they circulate to the point of cliché, in the process becoming almost completely emptied of content. There has even been some interest in the use of psychogeography as a research method for business research, where it is used to develop an expanded perspective on how organizations are experienced.[8] The dérive is reduced to a leisurely stroll, perhaps accompanied by some secondary musings about the nature of the spectacle, a dash of literary activity, with some local history thrown in for good measure.[9] This process is of course a hollowing out of the concept. Psychogeography for the Situationists was primarily not an aesthetic activity, but more than anything a strategic approach to understanding the forces shaping the city and from those finding points of intervention within it. At times, it verged on a nearly military framework, working to gain an intuitive understanding of the territory and its layering of images, affects, and circuits of capitalist valorization.[10]

Today we find ourselves in a condition of ever intensified spectacular sociability: all life put to work in webs of biopolitical production, overwhelming communicative and media flows, and the reshaping of the metropolis through culture-led gentrification. More than ever, well-developed psychogeographic investigations are needed to comprehend the shaping of the metropolis and the possibilities this offers for political action. But this is not a task for the carefree wanderings of the flâneur. Perhaps it is better suited for what Ian Sinclair has described as the superseding figure of the stalker, the one who knows where he is going, but not why or how.[11]

Against this emptied out conception of psychogeography we pose the idea that there are two, if not more, key strategies that it contains. The first would be to enact a process of de-familiarization from the routines and relationships to everyday life. Georg Simmel suggested well over a century ago that the intensity of experience found in the metropolis tended to stimulate a kind of blasé attitude from its inhabitants, one developed in order to protect oneself from overstimulation.[12] This is because confronted with the vast complexity and speed of everyday interactions, to engage fully with all of them would require all of one's mental resources and energies, if not more than they are capable of. A great deal of social routines and interactions are based around finding ways to deal with and work through this otherwise overwhelming complexity. In many ways, the arguments Simmel made a century ago could easily be argued to be just as relevant in the conditions of contemporary spectacular capitalism, and even more so with the intensification of communication and media flows.[13]

Psychogeography, through the practice of drifting, or the dérive, is a method of breaking from this formulaic interaction with the everyday. It is an attempt to bring to conscious attention all the dynamics and patterns of attraction and repulsion with the environment that remained submerged by routine relationships to the everyday. The dérive becomes a way that getting lost, of opening up how one is affected by the world, brings to the fore all the richness (and horror) of the everyday that is typically not paid attention to. In some ways, psychogeography could be understood to be an extension of how the Surrealists drew from psychoanalytic ideas in their exploration of the unconscious, creativity, and desire. As Andy Merrifield comments on the practice:

> As they shifted in and out of public spaces, they were intent on accumulating rich qualitative data, grist to their 'psychogeographical' mill, documenting odors and tonalities of the cityscape, its unconscious rhythms and conscious melodies: ruined façades, foggy vistas of narrow, sepia-soaked streets, nettle-ridden paving stones, empty alleyways at 3am., menace and mayhem, separation and continuity.[14]

The difference with psychogeography is that the terrain in question is not an individual mind, but rather the substrate of subconscious elements dispersed through the territory of the metropolis. In this way, it is inherently much more a social practice.

This 'getting lost to find the world again' is the aspect of psychogeography which is more readily grasped in the continued reception and circulation of Situationist ideas and practices. But what tends to get lost in this reception is the second and more directly strategic aspect of psychogeography, which is the emphasis on what new political opportunities these practices open up and make possible. For the SI, psychogeography was not simply valuable in itself as some sort of phenomenological investigation, or even as a sociological research method. Rather, its focus was to understand the ways in which the continued accumulation of capital were shaping the nature of the city, and thus affecting their relationship with the environment and the structuring of the everyday. And from this understanding of changes in value production and accumulation, the rendering of surplus for capital accumulation, it was thought to then be possible to find new ways to interrupt this ordering of the everyday and its avenues of exploitation. The dérive and psychogeography are thus forms of reconnaissance, gathering information of the territory in which tactics of everyday resistance are to unfold.

McKenzie Wark develops an interesting strategic appreciation of psychogeography, arguing that it sought to pose a form of lived time that does not accept the binary division between work and leisure.[15] This division between work and non-work time is accepted both by labor and capital, where it is in the interest of capital to extend and intensify the workday, and in the interest of labor to shorten it (or at least extract higher wages). It is often this shared focus on productivity that functions as a point of mediation between apparently conflicting interests, one in which the apparent representatives of working class struggles end up taking on a more of an accommodating function to the needs of capital.[16] Wark suggests that the Letterists and the SI started from a different conception of time, one "resolutely based on non-work."[17] This can be seen in what Debord considered his first major work, the painting of the slogan "Never work!" on a Parisian wall, a theme that was carried on through the activities of the SI. Here we can see a close, resonant connection with themes developed by the Italian autonomists, who likewise argued not just for reduction of working hours or higher wages, but for the abolition of work altogether.

Thus, for Wark the dérive becomes "the practice of lived time, time not divided and accorded a function in advance, a time inhabited neither by workers nor consumers."[18] But here we can also see what prospect the SI posed for capital despite themselves, in the ways this collapse of work and non-work, of play and labor, forms the basis of new patterns of work and capital accumulation. In some ways all the creative industries hype around new media could itself be understood as a perverse form of the SI's dream to completely collapse together art, play, labor, and everyday life. The key aspect missing from this, though, is the abolition of capitalism. To collapse work and leisure without an abolition of capitalism, without a complete transformation of everyday life, is to reinscribe the problems of alienated labor at a deeper level of subjectivation. As Andy Merrifield argues, "work-as-fun justifies non-stop toil, dreaming of riches and stock options, of hot dot.com start-ups, where hippie 20-some-things play Frisbee while they put in eighteen-hour days."[19]

This is not to cast blame on the SI by any means, for it is clear on many levels they were aware of this dynamic, even if not the particular forms it would take. Rather, it is to suggest that the SI's methods were formed in relationship to a moment of capitalist development. Thus, it is necessary to see how they could be adapted to the changing situations of the present. The use of psychogeography to open and defamiliarize the world, and from there to develop new political tools, remains a useful and productive approach

– as long as it understood that doing could (and likely should) reach different conclusions and understanding precisely because of the shift in the political terrain, the nature of capitalism, and so forth. A desire to collapse work and play into a new version of the everyday doesn't mean the same thing where that has already occurred, but as a method to intensify and extend the workday. Nonetheless, the practices that the SI proposed for investigating the everyday, their dérives and psychogeography, retain their value as ways to approach these transformed conditions, albeit it differently. A renewed form of psychogeographic practice could be benefit greatly from drawing on the autonomist class composition analysis.

Open Composition & Autonomous Inquiries

In the Situationist approach to psychogeography there is a two-way movement of opening up a terrain of struggle in order to sketch a new map of political subjectivation, but one that does so without foreclosing possible directions for future mutations in that form of politics. When the SI began their investigations into the changing psychogeographic nature of the city, they could not have figured in advance what kind of political practices would emerge from these investigations. If pressed in the late 1950s and early 1960s when they were most heavily using these techniques to make a prediction about what directions a radical political movement would take it, it is very unlikely (nearly impossible) that they would have imagined in advance the events of May 1968 and the alliance between the student and workers' movements. Very likely, given their intellectual and political background, they would have been much more focused on an expansion and radicalization of the existing labor movement, and on the role that forms of artistic (and anti-artistic) practice could have in this expansion, rather than considering student politics as a possible detonator or catalyst of a larger social explosion. But the benefit of the approach employed is that it remained open to possibilities that could not have been foreseen in advance, and even managed to prepare tools for political actors that could have not been anticipated. The eruption of spring 1968 saw the practice of occupations come to constitute a political territory in itself, from which other modes of being in the city, forms of life, and desire emerged.

This dual sense of finding spaces for a new politics but keeping them open to the unforeseen can be compared to the autonomist notions of technical and political class composition. Roughly speaking, technical composition is the forms of skills, knowledge, and abilities found within a given labor process. Political composition is the subjective experiences and possibilities for political transformation held by the working class at a given point. Clearly there is a close relationship between these two, but it is not one where either side can be understood in a reductive way. The autonomists understood very clearly that the working class is always more than its position in the overall labor process;[20] it is constantly overflowing and exceeding its enforced position with more desires, potentials, and directions than could ever be contained within that class relationship – whether this be for escape, security, or revolution.

In practice, what the autonomist notion and analysis of class did was to open up and expand the notion of class itself. While more traditional party-based forms of Marxism remained fixated on the industrial working class (such as the French and Italian communist parties), or basically factory workers, as the anticipated political subject, autonomists expanded their focus and understanding. While this initially began by trying to work from and with the eruption of wildcat factory strikes, these struggles subsequently and quickly spilled beyond the factory gates into the fabric of the city itself, as well as the university. There were intense struggles of the student movement, over healthcare and housing; the feminist movement put forth a very strong challenge to the notion of what counted as work by raising the question of gendered labor and social reproduction. While it might be tempting to understand all these 'new social movements' as being something quite different from the labor movement, at least in the traditional sense, at its best the autonomists understood these movements not as something distinct or opposed to working class movements, but as an extension of them. This is due in large part to the key concept of the social factory, where capital has developed to a point where it attempts to extend its control all throughout the social fabric. A consequence of this argument is that struggles occurring outside the factory gates still occur within the larger process of the factory-ization of society, and are thus still part of contesting the production of surplus value.

A class composition analysis thus asks questions about the expanded forms of social labor existing within the social factory. What are the labors that keep the social factory operating? What forms of value are created within this expanded mode of accumulation? What territories exist within it, and how are they shaped by their position within circuits of accumulation? The autonomist method to investigating these questions took the form of a workers' inquiry. Originally conceived of by Marx as a way to investigate factory conditions in the late 19th century, this was adapted and configured to the needs of the Italian situation. This was an approach that drew heavily from sociology and industrial relations to explore the changing nature of work conditions. A key aspect involves starting from the realization that often times the needs, desires, and conditions of workers' are not actually known – and cannot be presumed in advance. This is especially the case for a situation such as Italy in the 1950s to 1970s, which was undergoing profound and dramatic economic and social transformations.

The purpose of a workers' inquiry, however, was not a strictly sociological one. Its goal was not to map out and understand new configurations of class and power in a disinterested manner.

Rather, it was to work from within the forms of discontent that presented themselves, and to find ways to intensify their antagonisms, and to formulate new politics based upon them. The language used to describe this process was often quite abrasive, where someone like Mario Tronti would argue for a formulation of a partisan inquiry into conditions, a purely one-sided investigation founded on class hatred. This was far from the supposedly objective and politically neutral form of social science the autonomists frequently drew from, in addition to Marxist thought and politics.

In some ways, these are much the same questions the Situationists investigated through their practices. In both cases, what we see are approaches that are opening up to new forms of political practice outside the boundaries of traditional leftist politics, outside the activities of the union and the political party. Both Situationists and the autonomists are seeking to understand the changing terrain of politics and capital accumulation, and from that understanding to tease out possibilities for new political subjects. There are numerous ways that one could tease out how both approaches understand their situation using different but roughly comparable concepts.

For instance, the autonomist concept of the social factory (as well as the idea of real subsumption) is in many ways roughly comparable to the Situationists' concept of the spectacle, in so far as it expresses a new mode of capitalist accumulation, where the entire society is mediated through the production of imagery as surplus value. Psychogeographic practice can be understood as an investigation into the changing conditions of the city, which was also the goal and focus of class composition analysis in its approach to investigating the condition of labor in the social factory. Both traditions focused on investigating conditions within a social terrain, the changing conditions of capital accumulation, and what new strategies for contestation could be found within these conditions. A further consideration of how these approaches might be jointly used would be valuable for finding new tools for sabotage within the metropolitan factory.

Sabotage within the metropolitan factory

In recent autonomist writings, there has been a greater focus on the city understood as a kind of productive space in itself, or a kind of metropolitan factory.[21] Likewise, there has been a focus put on the city as a space of struggle within radical political thought more generally, which can be seen in ideas such as claiming a "right to the city," which emerges directly from the writing of Henri Lefebvre.[22] For the autonomist tradition, and those picking up and adapting its conceptual framework, the approach to the changing nature of the city is more particular; it brings together the changing conditions of dispersed forms of labor with the changing nature of political practice and social movement formations. This can be seen most clearly in the writings of Hardt and Negri, who argue that the modern metropolis is to multitude what the factory was to the working class: a primary site for the production of the working class, its internal encounters and organization, and for the expression of antagonism and rebellion. As opposed to this bounding of the productive space within the factory walls, Hardt and Negri suggest that the "contemporary productive activities of the multitude, however, overflow the factory walls to permeate the entire metropolis, and in the process the qualities and potential of those activities are transformed fundamentally."[23]

These productive activities are not just forms of labor as traditionally understood, but also the varied instances of affective and immaterial labor, artistic and creative practices, and all the dispersed flows of labor which exceed the boundaries of any particular capitalist organization but are becoming all the more essential to the reproduction of capital.[24] Even within traditional management and organization analysis, this poses a problem of capitalist discipline, in that firms are forced to rely upon the free self-organized activities of workers whose labor they do not directly control but rely upon.

In marketing practice and management this problem is addressed through the framework of the "co-creation" of value, where it is understood that the active participation of consumers, their circuits of feedback and creation, are directly productive of value. But the difficulty here is that "the interactive and interdependent nature of value co-creation processes challenges traditional management practices... Value co-creation requires an ability to engage 'the extended enterprise' by managing across and within customer and supplier value creation processes."[25] Here we can also see a perverse echo of some SI themes, where the emphasis of active participation (as opposed to the notion of spectatorship or passivity) is embraced, but not as a tool for liberating or bringing about new forms of political composition and subjectivity, but rather organizing a free labor force for the purposes of marketing and branding. This vast reservoir of free labor is all the more valuable in how it is often not even recognized as work, how it is both pleasurable and embraced by people even while being rendered into vast sums of revenue through social media and digital marketing.[26] It was the new economy's new 'hidden abode' of labor, one that has spread out beyond the circuits of both the high-tech and cultural economy.[27]

It is this conjunction and changed value production that bringing together psychogeography and class composition analysis in a more concerted way can help to address. The Situationists investigated ways that the accumulation of capital transformed the environments on multiple levels, from the physical shaping of space to the mental and emotional environments. When capital has extended its circuits of valorization through the city in much more pronounced ways, for instance by orienting around creative industries and city policies, the shaping of the city is embedded directly within the changing circuits of capital accumulation. One downside of the SI's approach was that its totalizing analysis left little room for appreciating more subtle differences in transformation of capital accumulation. Once the spectacularization of the everyday life and the city had been declared, it left little room for appreciating the changing nature of the spectacular forms sociability was taking. In this sense the practices of the dérive and psychogeography, which are much more connected with the earlier phases of the SI's activities, provide a better framework for analyzing the shifting configurations of everyday life then the more brazen and charismatic analyses that they are well known for.

The purpose of bringing together autonomist class composition analysis and psychogeography would be to develop an approach for drifting through and understanding the new territories of value accumulation in the city configured as a factory space. What are the possibilities for political recomposition within these circuits? If capital is drawing from an expanded terrain of value production that relies upon immense amounts of free labor, what possibilities are there for disrupting accumulation within these spaces? And perhaps even more importantly (even if somewhat dispiritingly), what the processes and dynamics that are blocking moments of political recomposition? While there has been a great deal of discussion about the inherent radical nature and social cooperation found within some forms of immaterial labor, often it seems that these have not led to the kind of political outcomes or collectivity emerging from them that one might have expected. The basin of immaterial labor, far from bursting forth with new communist militants, rather seem to be inhabited by people who might seem to be characterized by high degree of possessive individualism, more concerned about the nature of their practice, and with the very real questions of surviving within the challenging conditions of the city itself, more so then with questions of collective conditions of struggles. Perhaps it might be that their position within circuits of labor and reproduction tends to block, or preclude forms of collectivity from emerging, as Franco 'Bifo' Berardi has suggested.[28] But if this is the case, then what is needed is a closer investigation of the dynamics through which these blockages occur in order to sabotage the process.

There are a number of projects that are developing an approach along the lines of what has been proposed so far. This is not to suggest that they are ideal moments by any means, but rather develops practices that go in useful directions. One could look the activities of Precarias a la Deriva [PAD], who are a Madrid-based feminist collective, formed in 2002 in response to the call for a general strike. For women working in part-time and precarious work, the proposal of going on strike did not make sense. What would it mean to go on strike in those conditions? How could they do so without undercutting their own conditions of survival? How would it be possible to go on strikes over conditions of care work? PAD thus carried about drifts within the circuits of gendered labor and social reproduction they were enmeshed in. In this sense the dérive became not a tool for investigating the overall metropolis, but rather particular circuits and spaces within the city, and how they were being transformed: a tool for mapping out ones own working conditions, networks of support and relations. And most importantly, searching for what kind of politics, what kind of agency, or active refusals, are possible from within these positions.[29]

The Countercartographies Collective (or 3Cs) are a project based in North Carolina that has drawn from the history of mapping and autonomist politics to analyze the changing shape of academic labor. Similar to PAD's formation in response to a labor politics that did not seem adequate to the conditions of the present, 3Cs formed to investigate what kind of labor politics might be possible within the space of edufactory.[30] What flows of labor, resources, and collective intelligence existing within the university space? More recently, they carried out a mapping of these flows in relation to Queen Mary University in London, particularly focusing questions of labor and migration. This project included developing a board game that could be used as a pedagogic-political tool.[31] How might the different forms of labor and social life within the university, from adjuncts to janitors, students to tenured professors, relate to each other in a manner that could create common grounds of understanding and political action?

The practices of walking and drifting have been taken up in a much different way by the Walking Archives, an Argentinean project of art history coordinated by Eduardo Molinari, mapping that traces the continuing legacy of colonial power and domination. In particular, with their project *The Soy Children*,[32] the goal became to map out unseen social and economic relationships that were having immense impact on the environment. For instance, the ways in which the biotech economy, particularly through the production of genetically modified soy crops, could be shown to have immense impacts on culture and politics in Argentina far beyond agriculture. Molinari suggests that the biotechnological approach of genetic recombination has directly filtered through into transforming modes of cultural production and politics, creating new circuits for the operations of political and economic power: "today's neoliberalism needs a transgenic culture."[33] *The Walking Archives* then draws from psychogeographic practices such as the dérive, combined with archival investigations and curating of artistic events, and trace out these networks of power and influence and make them visible.[34]

In the UK, the Precarious Workers Brigade / Carrot Workers Collective have been organizing for several years on issues of precarity within cultural and creative work, particularly focusing on the questions of unpaid cultural labor in the forms of internships. This has taken multiple forms, from working with graduating art students warning them about the conditions they might likely face when entering the creative industries, which led to the production of a counter internship guide,[35] to the coordination of a peoples' tribunal on the question of precarious labor. While there has been much more focus on the question of unpaid labor, both within the cultural industries and more broadly,[36] the activities of PWB are distinct in that they are not formed around a legalistic claiming of rights. Rather, PWB attempts to create spaces for political recomposition, of open subjectivation through the conditions of shared precarity, rather than through attempting nostalgically to reclaim the position of some lost golden past for creative workers that was ensured through state protection.

What is clear from these brief examples is that the forms that political recomposition would take within the metropolitan factory are significantly different from those employed within industrial struggles previously. Organizing around arts and cultural labor, in circuits of immaterial work, would necessitate a different approach – in the same way the call for a general strike might not be the best tactic for precarious workers. The conditions of creative labor within the metropolis are often times extremely individualizing and isolating, where freelance workers find themselves moving from café to café, project to project, with no common space that they encounter others facing the similar conditions. The purposes of bringing together psychographic drifts with class composition analysis is not to propose in advance any particular tactics for countering these conditions – rather it is to suggest that not enough is known about the particularities and compositions of these situations – and that any radical politics worthy of the name must begin from working within and against them.

Conclusion

In one of the few exhibitions staged by the Situationists, Guy Debord wrote over the painting of fellow SI member Pinot Gallizio, "Abolition du travail aliene" (Abolition of alienated labor). Mikkel Bolt Rasmussen argues that this could serve as a bit of mantra for the SI, that the creativity "the artist was endowed with in bourgeois society had to be set free and generalized."[37] In this sense, it was not all that paradoxical that the SI both celebrated and despised the role of the artist. It was not so much that they were opposed to the existence of creative practice, play, or imagination at all – for this is exactly what they wanted to expand all throughout everyday life in revolutionary directions. But this is precisely their objection to the restricted role of creativity within the figure of the artist (although the same could be said of the restrictive role of the creative class or cultural industries). For the SI, art had to be realized throughout the everyday and not just within the separate realm of the art world.

In the conditions of neoliberal post-Fordist capitalism fueled by creativity, play, and desire, art has indeed moved beyond the separate realm of the art world. Unfortunately, the effects of this artistic sublation have been somewhat less than liberatory. In these conditions, it no longer makes sense to make recourse to play and creativity in the same way, assuming that liberating them will drastically transform everyday life. In reality, it is precisely a continued attachment to such claims that may bind people even tighter to their own domination. The task of finding new methods for contesting neoliberal capitalism starts not from continually recycling the ideas of previous revolutionary movements without adapting them to the current conditions. Rather, it starts from understanding how the demands of previous movements have shifted patterns of life and labor – and by drifting through this metropolitan factory and its circuits of valorization, finds new ways to sabotage these very circuits

Notes

1. Chtcheglov, Ivan (1981 [1953]) "Formulary for a New Urbanism," *Situationist International Anthology.* Ken Knabb, Ed. Berkeley: Bureau of Public Secrets: 1-4. Available at http://www.bopsecrets.org/SI/Chtcheglov.htm.

2. As Dardot and Lavel put it, "Neoliberalism is not merely destructive of rules, institutions and rights. It is also *productive* of certain kinds of social relations, certain ways of living, certain subjectivities. In other words, at stake in neo-liberalism is nothing more, nor less, than the *form of our existence* – the way in which we are led to conduct ourselves, to relate to others and to ourselves." (2014: 3).

3. Fleming, Peter and Carl Cederstrom (2012) *Dead Man Working.* Winchester: Zero Books.

4. Lucas, Rob (2010) "Dreaming in Code," *New Left Review* Number 62: 125-132. See also Hassan and Purser (2007).

5. Boltanski, Luc and Eve Chiapello (2005) *The New Spirit of Capitalism.* London: Verso.

6. Colectivo Situaciones (2011) *19&20: notes on a new social protagonism.* Wivenhoe: Minor Compositions.

7. For more on this, see Hearn (2010) and Ealham (2010).

8. Knowles, Deborah (2009) "Claiming the Streets: Feminist Implications of Psychogeography as a Business Research Method," *The Electronic Journal of Business Research Methods* Volume 7 Issue 1: 47-54. See also Vains (2008)

9. Baker, Phil (2003) "Secret City: Psychogeography and the End of London," *London from Punk to Blair.* Joe Kerr & Andrew Gibson, Eds. London: Reaktion Books: 323-333.

10 For more on this see Chapter 3 in Shukaitis, Stevphen (2016) *The Composition of Movements to Come: Aesthetics & Cultural Labor After the Avant-Garde.*

11 Sinclair, Ian (1997) *Lights Out for the Territory.* London: Granta Books.

12 Simmel, Georg (1950) "The Metropolis and Mental Life," *The Sociology of Georg Simmel.* New York: Free Press: 409-424.

13 Gilman-Opalsky, Richard (2011) *Spectacular Capitalism: Guy Debord and the Practice of Radical Philosophy.* London: Minor Compositions.

14 Merrifield, Andy (2005) *Guy Debord.* London: Reaktion Books, 31.

15 Wark, McKenzie (2011) *The Beach Beneath the Streets.* London: Verso.

16 Seidman, Michael (1990) *Workers Against Work: Labor in Paris and Barcelona during the Popular Fronts.* Berkeley: University of California Press.

17 Wark (2005), 25.

18 Ibid., 25.

19 Merrifield (2005), 140.

20 Carlsson, Chris (2008) *Nowtopia.* Oakland: AK Press.

21 For the underpinning of this concept see Negri (2006), Hardt and Negri (2009), Pasquinelli (2009), and Plan B Bureau (2009).

22 Harvey, David (2012) *Rebel Cities: From the Right to the City to the Urban Revolution.* London: Verso.

23 Hardt, Michael and Antonio Negri (2009) *Commonwealth.* Cambridge: Harvard University Press, 250.

24 As Helen Molesworth describes it, "There is an almost uncanny homology between Hardt and Negri's assessment of our current economic transformations and the strategies deployed by artists negotiating the ramifications of labor's prior transformation. Artists who play out the roles of both manager and worker

in task based and process works render the logic of industrial production into aesthetic information. Artists who mime the structure of management both creatively and routinely manipulate information... And artists who turn to the viewer to complete the world consistently do so in a bodily and affective mode" (2003: 47).

25 Payne, Adrian, Kaj Storbacka, and Pennie Frow (2008) "Managing the co-creation of value," *Journal of the Academy of Marketing Science* 36, 93.

26 For more on this, see Terranova (2004) and Zwick et al. (2008).

27 Bohm, Steffen and Chris Land (2012) "The new "hidden abode": reflections on value and labour in the new economy," *Sociological Review* Volume 60 Number 2: 217-240.

28 Berardi, Franco (2009) *Precarious Rhapsody*. London: Minor Compositions.

29 Precarias a la Deriva (2006) A Very Careful Strike – Four Hypotheses. *The commoner* no 11: 33-45.

30 For more on this, see Casas-Cortes and Cobarrubias (2007) and Edufactory (2009).

31 Countermapping Queen Mary Collective (2012) Universities in Question: Countermapping the university. *Lateral*. Available at http://lateral.culturalstudiesassociation.org.

32 Molinari, Eduardo (2012) *Walking Archives: The Soy Children*. Wivenhoe: Minor Compositions.

33 Ibid., 5.

34 See also Molinari (2011) and Mayo (2012).

35 Precarious Workers Brigade (2012) Free labour syndrome. Volunteer work or unpaid overtime in the creative and cultural sector. In E. Armano and A. Murgia (Eds.) *Mappe della precarietà vol. II: Knowledge workers, creatività, saperi e dispositivi di soggettivazione*. Bologna: I libri di Emil: 51-65.

36 For more on this, see Gil and Pratt (2008, Ross (2009), and Standing (2011).
37 Rasmussen, Mikkel Bolt (2011) "To Act in Culture While Being Against All Culture: The Situationists and the Destruction of RSG-6," *Expect Anything Fear Nothing: The Situationist Movement in Scandinavia and Elsewhere*. Copenhagen and Brooklyn: Nebula / Autonomedia, 98.

The Factory of Individuation

[T]he position of the artist in our society is exactly that of an assembly line worker in Detroit. – Carl Andre

In this epigraph, the well-known conceptual artist and sculptor Carl Andre, a founding member of the Art Workers Coalition in 1969, makes a bold claim about the position and status of the artist, and of artistic labor, in society.[1] There is a strong temptation to dismiss such a statement as hyperbole, but if one moves past this reaction, his claim poses a number of questions. Is Andre talking about artistic labor as occupying a position subordinate to the demands of capital accumulation? Is artistic labor, subject to capitalist discipline, analogous to the position of the working class within the capitalist labor process? Given that throughout his life Andre identified with labor politics, both ideologically and aesthetically (he dressed like a clichéd image of the factory worker), is he suggesting here that artists could occupy the revolutionary position that Marxist analysis ascribes to the proletariat, the universal class capable of abolishing class distinctions (and, thereby, itself), thus bringing about a new society? Is Andre considering how creativity and imagination would come to play an increasingly vital role in the broader processes of economic production?[2]

Perhaps it is too much to hang all of these questions on a single quotation taken out of context. Still, Andre clearly gestures to the ambivalent location of and role that artistic labor plays within social, political, and organizational analysis. As Julia Bryan-Wilson observes in her excellent history of the Art Workers Coalition and the figures emerging out of it, Andre himself was somewhat ambivalent in his identification, proclaiming his connection with labor in more of a formal than practical manner – foregrounding labor while disavowing it.³ This ambivalence, however, is far from unique, and it seems to characterize the position of artistic and cultural labor more generally, as a newly exalted practice that not only brings with it political possibilities and the potential for renewed economic growth but also threatens exploitation and precarity.⁴

We were reminded of this identification of the artist with the factory worker when walking through the weekend markets situated in the former Truman Brewery in east London's Brick Lane.⁵ Here one can see an almost perfect illustration of the image Andre might have been trying to summon. Brick Lane provides an example of a former industrial space – a large brewery taking up almost nineteen acres – that was shut down during the 1980s. Since then, the space has been used for myriad purposes: parking for workers going to the financial district, studio spaces, and a weekend market for cultural and artistic products, food, music, and clothing. Here, the identification of the artist with the factory worker has reached an almost overly literal conclusion: the factory space has been emptied out but filled again with independent cultural producers selling their wares. One could suggest that it is a perfect example of what Sharon Zukin described as the "artistic mode of production."⁶

Is the factory space being replaced by cultural and creative industries? Or is this shift an illusion, as the number of people selling their own work and craft is quantitatively small? The small proportion of independent cultural producers in markets like Brick Lane does not stop such sites from being narrated and represented as spaces where independent artists and crafts people operate. What occurs in the organization of the cultural labor process amid these changing conditions? What happens to cultural workers in the creative factory? What is the effect of the apparent lack of direct managerial control on their labor processes?

Our desire to answer these kinds of questions, in light of statements by Zukin, Andre, and others, led us to develop the Metropolitan Factory project,⁷ a survey, and series of interviews based on Karl Marx's 1880 "A Worker's Inquiry" and adapted to investigate the conditions and activities of independent cultural producers in markets like Brick Lane. Rather than focus on macrosocial questions about the rise of the creative class, a topic that has been explored widely and from a wide array of perspectives, this chapter focuses on the portion of our findings that relates to the micropolitics of cultural labor in the metropolitan factory. As the composition of the labor process shifts towards higher levels of self-organization, how are workers affected? How is their relationship to their own labor process impacted? And how does the dynamic of what Melissa Gregg has described as "work's intimacy,"[8] the increasing subjective investment of an individual in the self-managed labor process, shift the grounds and possibility of a labor politics?

Workers' Inquiry in the Metropolitan Factory

> The metropolis is to the multitude what the factory was to the industrial working class. The factory constituted in the previous era the primary site and posed the conditions for three central activities of the industrial working class: its production; its internal encounters and organization; and its expressions of antagonism and rebellion. The contemporary productive activities of the multitude, however,

> overflow the factory walls to permeate the entire metropolis, and in the process the qualities and potential of those activities are transformed fundamentally. – Michael Hardt and Antonio Negri[9]

The aim of our project was to illuminate the area of knowledge about the lived realities of creative workers; as Mark Banks has rightly pointed out, despite the vast proliferation of publications on creative industries and creative labor, relatively little is known about creative workers as workers *per se*. While the cultural labor process has been discussed in terms of its broader impacts, approached philosophically and managerially, there has been less of a concern with the concrete specifics of creative labor as a labor *process*, at least compared to the detailed analyses of industrial labor that one finds in the history of industrial sociology and labor studies. This, for Banks, is a misstep. He argues for an analysis of the politics of cultural work rooted in the conditions of the cultural labor process, or, more specifically, "within the industrialization process of cultural production... how it is constructed, managed, and performed."[10]

In order to do this, Banks discusses three general approaches to the politics of cultural work: that of Critical Theory and the Frankfurt School, the neo-Foucauldian approach focusing on questions of governmentality, and the liberal democratic celebration of potential. Each of these approaches is useful, drawing attention to aspects of cultural work that it would be a mistake to neglect. For instance, while it might be easy for critical writing on cultural work to dismiss arguments about the democratizing potential and creation of meaning and worth within cultural work, doing so discards some main rationales and values that people involved in forms of cultural work rely on to explain the importance of what they are doing (to themselves and to others). Insofar as critical scholarship focuses on developing an ongoing relationship with cultural workers, as well as understanding the politics of cultural work, it is important not to discard such understandings as ideological covers for the realities of self-exploitation, even if they sometimes appear to be. For example, Banks examines the ways in which precarious cultural workers are themselves "actively implicated in reproducing enterprise values through their own strategies of economizing," even as those values undermine the security and conditions of these workers precisely because they appear "to provide the only means for establishing the precarious rewards that are being offered."[11] This is precisely what we focus on here, moving away from more sectoral-level analyses and toward what might be called the micropolitics of work – that is, we focus on the spaces where cultural workers make these ambivalent kinds of justifications and balance the costs and libidinal investments of imagination, meaning, and desire.

If we know relatively little about cultural workers as workers, then we know even less about cultural workers as managers and as *their own* managers, which is to say, as the administrators of themselves as forms of self-activating entrepreneurial capital – precisely the organizational and subjective form called for by current conditions of cultural labor in the metropolis. If creative workers are required to organize themselves into what Angela McRobbie[12] has described as microstructures, where risk is individualized and shifted on to the worker, how does this change the relationship of these workers to both their labor process and the process of organizing their work? More than a decade ago, McRobbie identified this shifting of risk as one way that the speeding up of cultural labor leads to the decline of political culture; these processes have only intensified since then.[13]

We approach the issues outlined above from an autonomist approach, drawing on debates in contemporary theory and politics around the nature of immaterial and affective labor.[14] Hardt and Negri intimate this approach in the epigraph above, arguing that the role formerly played by the factory in the production and experience of the working class for the multitude is now being played by the metropolis itself. Productive activity today is no longer confined to particular spaces or times – such as the bounded walls of the factory or the regular workday – but rather flows through the entire space of the city and its sociality. David Harvey discusses this point in his recent work, suggesting that "the concept of work has to shift from a narrow definition attaching to industrial forms of labor to the far broader terrain of the work entailed in the production and reproduction of an increasingly urbanized daily life."[15] This shifting is readily the case for cultural workers in the markets off Brick Lane. While it might seem that cultural workers have filled the space of the factory with new forms of labor, their work extends far beyond the space of the market. The metropolis has itself been transformed by these shifts in the arrangements of working lives, which is partially grasped by discussions about the rise of the creative class and the creative city.[16] As Allen Scott has argued, there is an intimate connection between urbanization and capitalist development; every historical form of capitalism is associated with a distinctive type of city. He presents a three-stage typology of transition, a model that corresponds closely to the area around Brick Lane. It begins with nineteenth-century urbanization based on tightly-knit spaces of factories and cheap tract housing, followed by a second machine age characterized by mass production and the extension of the metropolitan zones, with development of white- and blue-collar areas. In the third machine age, which encompasses the 1970s to the present, the rise of computer and information technologies underpin the development of the cognitive-cultural economy. The cognitive-cultural economy is "marked by the increasingly flexible and malleable systems of production… that are now so strongly present at the leading edges of the contemporary economy… The reasons for the attraction of cognitive-cultural industries to locations in the city reside primarily in the organizational logic of the new economy generally."[17]

While these debates have been quite fruitful in bringing new perspectives to the realities of cultural work, they could likewise be critiqued for lacking a degree of caution and self-reflexivity in their analyses. For instance, autonomist analysis has at times fallen back into the overly positive celebration of cultural work that Banks identifies with liberal democratic analysis. At times, it has been argued that forms of immaterial labor and cultural work contain an almost inherent radical political potentiality because of the way that they organize and rely on collaboration and networks. One can look here to arguments put forth by Hardt and Negri that celebrate immaterial labor as a kind of "elementary communism."[18] While few other commentators have followed the implications of such a suggestion to its conclusion, there is a marked tendency to take on this kind of optimistic analysis of creative labor's potentials[19] and, more broadly, the possibilities contained in cognitive capitalism.[20]

But there is a problem with this style of analysis. Surely, if it were correct, then the former factory spaces of Brick Lane markets and surrounding areas, filled to the brink with cultural and artistic labor, should reveal some signs of communist organizing. And while one might very well encounter numerous Che Guevara images in these markets, the processes of countercultural consumption prevail, along with a supply of workers more intent on continuing to develop their individual projects and practices than on communizing the means of production or ending the reign of the bourgeoisie over social life.

That radical political outcomes have not manifested themselves, however, does not mean that the autonomist concepts and approaches are not valid and useful for further analysis and development. What it does show is that certain aspects of the functioning of cultural and creative work have not been fully appreciated by the autonomist approach and immaterial labor debates. For this reason we think it is especially important to pay attention to the arguments that focus on what Franco Berardi has described as the "dark side of immaterial labor,"[21] the dynamics that, far from creating possibilities for a new radical politics, actually work to undermine the spaces and processes of animating new collective subjects operating as a part "communicative capitalism."[22] It is equally important to consider what Peter Fleming and Carl Cederstrom have described as "dead men [and women] working,"[23] for whom the logic of work has taken over all aspects of life. The dark side of cultural work contains the negative repercussions of the forms of self-exploitation that are fueled by the desire for meaning and fulfillment in work. Here, the micropolitics of the cultural worker are formed and reformed: in the dreams of workers who have discovered that they are at work even as they sleep,[24] in awakening to the realization that they are further from achieving freedom and autonomy through liberation from work than they expected.[25]

In other words, the immaterial labor debate provides important tools for analyzing cultural labor but makes arguments that contrast with the lived realities of cultural workers. We argue for looking at material realities of cultural work by harkening back to earlier moments in autonomist theory and practice – returning to the history of workers' inquiry approach to see how it could be updated to investigate the conditions of contemporary cultural labor. Workers' inquiry has a long and varied tradition, stretching from Marx's proposal in *La Revue Socialiste* to survey working conditions, through to the development of industrial sociology carried out within labor struggles and communist militancy by groups such as the Johnson-Forrest Tendency and Socialisme ou Barbarie.[26] Workers' inquiry also played a major role in the development of dissident Marxism in Italy in the 1960s and 1970s.[27] In this case – with a desire to intensify and deepen rather than controlling or pacifying the social antagonisms – sociological approaches were deployed to understand the massive waves of worker militancy emerging outside and against the official party and union structures.

Workers' inquiry has thus varied significantly in its approach and methodologies. However, it was generally formed around several key ideas, such as not presuming too much in advance about labor conditions and that the tools of the social sciences can be put to use to build and strengthen radical politics. A key elaboration of workers' inquiry emerged, again during the 1960s and 1970s, when the approach shifted its focus to understanding the changing nature of class composition and how the current arrangement of the labor process (capital's technical composition) either made possible or served to block the forms of politics that working classes engaged, from refusing work to accommodation of capitalist demands (capital's political composition). In this sense, workers' inquiry is less about trying to create any fixed idea of class or the labor process than it is about trying to map out the forces at play within a given situation in such a way that they can be utilized to further develop political and social antagonisms. While more recent projects taking up and developing workers' inquiry have often varied significantly from versions elaborated in the 1970s (tending, for instance, to focus more on flexible forms of post-Fordist labor rather than on factories), there remains a core emphasis on social-sciences methods and approaches in the service of political struggles.[28] In the Metropolitan Factory project, we adapted ideas from these workers' inquiry practices to investigate current conditions of cultural labor and production, particularly as they depart from their celebrated positions within cultural policy and social theory.

The Factory that makes you, they say, it never stops

Of the themes that emerge in our discussions with cultural workers, one of the strongest concerned subjectivation at and through work, that is, the nature of attachment and relationship to the work itself. Cultural workers described their projects clearly and repeatedly not only as forms of work but also as expressions of a deep and personal essence: labor functioning as a form of authentic self-expression. For instance, the proprietor of a stall selling books and music hesitated to describe the endeavor as a business and, even when conceding the point, struggled to express how it could be best categorized as such: "I should really avoid categorization, because my stall is a representation of me." Participants often commented that operating a stall in the market as a business was desirable precisely because of the way it was an alternative to more traditional forms of waged employment. Thus, forms of what could easily be described as cultural entrepreneurship helped to articulate both a space through which cultural workers could operate and a logic of self-representation and subjectivation through that self-representation.[29]

Such near-total identification of one's self with one's labor resonates with Berardi's discussion of contemporary immaterial labor as putting the soul to work, instrumentalizing an intimate sense of self and identity through a project of cultural work.

In the interviews, a deep imbrication of the self in the cultural labor process played itself out in different ways. A designer of stuffed animals reported that customers with well-paid, albeit stressful, jobs (i.e., bankers and city workers) often told him they were jealous of the freedom and flexibility they assumed he possessed as a stallholder. This information raised some interesting questions. Are stressed city workers genuinely jealous of the autonomy and flexibility they attribute to cultural workers? And – regardless of whether that is true – do workers in the market perceive themselves as having good working conditions and thus occupying a desirable position?

Cultural workers on Brick Lane and the surrounding markets often described their projects as forming around personal ethics and values, ranging from the more obvious use of organic materials and sustainable practices to the infusion of a sense of humor, satire, philosophy, or other, less tangible, qualities into the projects themselves. The attempts to personalize cultural work were described as positive, both in the sense of making the work more meaningful for the producers and in the sense of creating and maintaining works of high quality and originality. Thus, it could be argued that the greater subjective investment of cultural producers was important not only for producers but also for the space itself, in that it was a way to differentiate the area and around Brick Lane from what one usually finds on a high street (although it is debatable how different it really is).

A sense of subjective investment is evident in a clothing designer's comment that a key requirement for getting involved in a project was not just to understand the ethos informing the work, but to possess a personality capable of conveying this: "It's not about just understanding, it's about having a personality. And giving someone the autonomy to be themselves and talk about the things they get excited about." This mirrors managerial strategies of putting one's personality to work in corporate environments[30] and resonates with the analysis put forward by Neff, Wissinger, and Zukin around the intertwining of entrepreneurial labor and identity work in media and cultural industries, both on and off the job, in a way that involves the acceptance of higher levels of risk and instability: the contemporary Faustian bargain required to work "cool jobs in hot industries."[31]

The Languages of Work

Given the profound subjective involvement of workers in their projects and overall labor processes and the increasing difficulty it poses to making clear distinctions between work and life, the question of the language used to frame these relations is both complicated and important. This poses a difficulty for research: if the point of the investigation is to explore the shifting boundaries between work and life, the necessity of framing the questions in certain ways almost inevitably skews the conversation in a specific direction. The concern is not that the framing will violate some positivist decorum or method, for indeed a significant element of workers' inquiry as an approach is formed around precisely abandoning the pretense (and very possibility) of social-scientific objectivity. We wanted to ask people what language they choose and use to describe their own practices, how they understand or frame them, particularly if they differentiated between forms of work they engage in to support themselves financially and the "creative" or "real" practices that motivate (but do not always materially sustain) them.

In one instance, someone who split labor time between practicing artistic photography and producing commercial stuffed animals described this division as having different rooms to work in, both literally and metaphorically. And when asked how the worker distinguished between the two practices, the answer depended on whom the conversation was with in terms of the vocabulary used and how the production of stuffed animals related to other activities. This question generated tension by juxtaposing the worker's self-description as an artist with the realization that the majority of laboring time was spent on the production of what the worker considered to be less artistic objects.

A blurring of the lines between profitable work, creative activity, and other (and often all) aspects of life was, perhaps unsurprisingly, a recurring theme of the study. For the most part, this lack of clear distinctions and boundaries did not seem to bother the creative workers themselves; it was, however, perceived by them as challenging for their significant others. The reported reasons for these frustrations varied from the difficulties in finding spare time or space unrelated to creative work (in one instance, artistic production and storage swallowed larger and larger swathes of shared housing) to the low or nonexistent income from certain forms of creative practice to the stresses caused by needing to balance the tensions between different forms of creative work.

The issue of balancing work and life commitments – even the suggestion that it was possible to distinguish between life and work and different types of work – almost became a point of comic relief. As one worker, whose time was split between artistic production and manufacturing garden statues out of chicken wire, commented: "I don't know when the work ends. I'm happy with that, I don't stress too much about there not being an edge." For our interviewees, the distinction between life and work seemed to be the hardest to make.

It was often the more creative or artistic elements that were most highly valued (by themselves) and experienced or "felt" less "like work," and thus it was much harder to draw any clear distinctions around them. This was particularly the case for small projects, where the same people undertook both creative and more administrative tasks. Workers described ways that they attempted to find a balance between their activities, but more often this fell back into a description of their (in)ability to make such distinctions.

Organization of the Labor Process

A further aspect of organizational strategies could be seen in the ways the production process was organized and separated from other times and places. Producers tended to state that they would attempt to designate some space exclusively for their work, whether this meant keeping materials in a particular part of the house or working from a studio or other space. Despite these attempts, the designated spaces often failed to contain their working activities, with the movement of work outside these spaces being alternatively celebrated ("I could work anywhere") or met with open resentment ("I end up working everywhere"). The high costs of space in places like London, particularly in areas that have been experiencing significant increases in rent, tend to push cultural producers back into working from home as they cannot afford another workspace. This tendency mirrors the history of cultural production in the area, for instance, of leather jackets and handbags, which originated in home-based production processes before (after a fair degree of success) production moved out of living areas and into separate work spaces. As Andrew Ross has argued, the effects of creative industries policies were mitigated by rising real estate prices, thus demonstrating that the one proven method of wealth generation around creative industries activities is through the increased values of rents and property.[32]

The dynamics and discussion surrounding such spatial boundaries were roughly mirrored in the ways that producers tended to organize their time. Any given time could potentially, and indeed often did, become part of work time. And, despite this tendency to convert all time into work time, the theme of distancing one's creative production from work as an imposition, as something not freely chosen, was maintained, such as when a designer commented, "So I just sort of keep going. But it never feels like a chore, I enjoy it. If I wasn't doing this as a business, I'd be doing this as a hobby." Some cultural producers at the market described how they preferred to continue working on production tasks while running their stalls because it helped fill the time that would otherwise be spent waiting for customers, which would then "feel more like work."

Cynthia Negrey has observed that, paradoxically, the workers with flexibility in both their schedule and location tend to experience overwork.[33] This follows from the logic that flexibility in work, the perceived or expected ability to work almost anywhere or anytime, coupled with the pressures of working in a highly competitive environment for cultural production, ensures that any available time becomes more work time. Through this subtle shift, attributes of creative labor and flexibility changed from something worth celebrating and embracing into a burden, and creative workers were condemned to be producing "freely" at all times.

The Future?

Shifts in the relationship between creative and private practices among our interviewees had varied impacts on their ability to develop, or even think about developing, a sense of long-term planning. The general disavowal of organizational matters as unfortunate of business often seemed to make questions of longer-term planning difficult to even approach. These disavowals ranged from the bookseller who declared his desire to "physically detach [himself] from the cruel reality of invoicing" to a more generally expressed dislike of the "business side of things." Organizational matters and planning were often described as important and necessary but at the same time not as desirable or enjoyable, even as their rejection tended to produce other constraints on projects and, more generally, livelihoods.

This aversion to planning resulted not only in constraints over what was or could be possible but also, at times, in a kind of paradoxical freedom. On the more negative side, the labor of international designers working in the margins of creative industries often did not generate the income, or at least officially declared income, necessary to secure and maintain visa status in the United Kingdom. This seemed contradictory, given that the markets around Brick Lane area exploit the image of a vibrant space offering goods from a variety of different cultures and styles – as opposed to the mass-manufactured imported goods sold elsewhere. Simultaneously, the pressures placed on creative workers in these smaller projects tend to encourage them to move elsewhere.

This lack of planning was often apparent into the way people described how they began working in the Brick Lane area. Frequently it was described as something that happened by accident or that they just fell into and ended up doing for a number of years. One designer described his work in these markets as coming out of a desire to take a certain kind of design practice and move it into broader circulation, to find "a way of putting graphics onto different types of canvas." But even then, that original impetus, coupled with the necessary labor of organizing production to support selling in the market, took on its own structure and ended up taking the time that would otherwise be spent working on the original project.

This example points to the dynamics of ambivalence and competing motivations inherent in self-organized forms of cultural work. Such forms of work are purported to offer a much greater (and highly celebrated) degree of flexibility and autonomy, but the onus of self-management simultaneously increases the workload and managerial tasks needed to maintain creative practices. One interviewee from a fashion firm commented that it is only after starting a creative company that one realizes "how little creativity there's going to be involved in it and actually how much there is to do with putting spreadsheets together, making sure you ordered the right amount of t-shirts, making sure you didn't overspend." This statement resonates with McRobbie's argument that people increasingly "have to become their own micro-structures, they have to do the work of structures by themselves" in a process that speeds up the workflow and relies on self-promotional strategies.[34] Indeed, some interviewees who reported being able to balance their artistic work with work they did to pay the bills felt that this very skill threatened to demystify the nature of artistic and cultural work.

This ambivalence, learned over years of experience working in these markets, seemed to most trouble cultural producers when they reflected on their work. Several interviewees commented that they could not be sure whether they had finally managed to work out a good arrangement for their creative practices and livelihoods, or whether they were rationalizing their situations. One artist described how he had come to realize that spending more time on work to pay bills than on artistic labor had created a healthier balance. The promised freedoms and autonomy of creative self-determined worth still managed to shine through as something important and valued, even through all the constraints and difficulties imposed by the realities of creative work. Or, as one of the artists in the market/on Brick Lane put it, "it might be illusory, but there is an element of self-determined, self-empowerment about it, which I think gets you through it".

The Iron Cage of Cultural Entrepreneurship

> Homo Economicus is an entrepreneur, an entrepreneur of himself. – Michel Foucault[35]

When art students graduate from their academies, they usually end up as "no-collar" workers in the industry by day and as artists by night in their dreams. Contemporary art can also be a refuge from the relentless pressures of the culture industry. But it is the kind of refuge that makes no bones about the fact that it is also a secret internal exile. – Raqs Media Collective, "How to be an artist at night"[36]

In his analysis of the shifting forms of neoliberalism in the United Kingdom (shared across political parties), Stuart Hall argued that the processes in question, far from being just an economic transformation, represented a much larger process of cultural transformation. For Hall, Thatcherism represented a radical remodeling of state and economy, an epochal shift through which "slowly but surely, everybody – even if kicking and screaming to the end – becomes his/her own kind of 'manager'."[37] This process of inculcating an entrepreneurial and managerial, or self-managerial, subjectivity can be seen clearly in the ways that cultural workers around markets in East London organize and relate to their work. This is precisely what Jason

Read gestures to, invoking Foucault, when he describes homo economicus an entrepreneur of himself.[38] Likewise, this is what the Raqs Media Collective describes in the form of the former art student who graduates into the no color workforce, a low paid wage worker during the day and an artist at night, in their dreams.

To suggest that neoliberalism has something to do with the development of an entrepreneurial subjectivity is, of course, not a new argument. A significant amount of recent, largely Foucauldian, scholarship examines this very process.[39] But it is also important to remember, as Andrew Ross has argued, that this remodeling of the economy and the "changing of men's souls" under neoliberalism is neither a simple nor an easy process; rather, "the reeducation of their sentiments was an arduous campaign that had to be waged day in, day out until neoliberal instincts like self-optimization were regarded as common sense."[40] This is what makes the analysis of these processes in relationship to artistic and cultural labor so necessary. While there might be degrees of greater resistance to neoliberalization in many aspects of social life, it is paradoxically often embraced more easily within artistic and cultural work; these workers are told (and tell themselves) that by taking on the practices of self-organization and flexibility in and through precarious conditions they will achieve a higher degree of autonomy and self-determination and thus create more livable situations for their particular practices. Kirsten Forkert has explored this recently, comparing the ways that the contexts of London and Berlin shape the possibilities open to cultural artistic workers.[41] As Neff, Wissinger, and Zukin have suggested, despite their aura of hipness, "new media workers and fashion models are really the Stakhanovites, or norm-making 'shock workers,' of the new economy... These workers now directly bear entrepreneurial risks previously mediated by the firm, such as business cycle fluctuations and market failures."[42]

To point this out is not to argue that the experiences, however ambivalent, of greater flexibility and control over work conditions described by cultural workers are necessarily an illusion or some form of false consciousness. It does mean, however, that the conditions of this work are more complicated and contradictory than one might expect, given the celebration of creative and cultural work within debates found in cultural policy and some sections of autonomist theory. And it does show the way, as Ricardo Antunes argues, that immaterial labor operates as the meeting point between labor-subjectivity and a productive process, where "collective apprenticeship becomes the principal of productivity."[43] Both the creative class and the multitude have been described as opening up new possibilities for social and political interaction, but a consideration of the concrete situations experienced by such workers tends to paint a more complicated and less rosy picture. The "artistic multitude" theorized by Pascal Gielen, though perhaps important to the development of the creative economy and innovation more broadly, seems entrapped within the cultural logic of its own creation.[44] Much as the realities of "actually existing socialism" departed significantly from expectations, the "actually existing elementary communism" of immaterial labor leaves something to be desired.

This chapter started off considering Andre's suggestion that the positions of the artist and the factory worker were largely the same. This is a debatable proposition, even for artistic and cultural workers who literally have moved their activities back into former factory spaces. The task of rebuilding a labor politics around mutating forms of immaterial and cultural labor, which our project attempts to do, requires a developed and in-depth engagement with the modes of subjectivation that occur through these forms of labor, not assumptions about how these forms of labor shape the experiences and expectations of workers. If Berardi is correct in his proposition that the soul has been put to work, then this putting to work has not resulted in anything like a great liberation of creativity or the creation of new forms of autonomy. Rather, it has encouraged the cultural workers discussed here to develop highly individuated forms of subjective investment that tend to block off and preclude collective reflections and struggles around their conditions. As Gigi Roggero writes, "the political composition of class is crushed within the sociological mold of its technical composition." Rebuilding and restarting a cycle of class and political recomposition needs to commence not with a mystified understanding of the conditions of cultural work, but through an understanding of what forms of politics are enabled and disabled by the shifting terrain of the labor process today.[45]

Notes

1   For some recent writing and analysis of the shifting relations between art and labor see Aranda, Wood, and Vidokle (2011); Diederichsen (2008); Klamer (1996); Abbing (2004); Sholette and Ressler (2013); Siebert and Wilson (2013); Siegelbaum (2013); Kálmán and Šević (2010); Wherry (2012); and Warsza (2017).

2   Similarly, it had previously been claimed that what was good for GM was good for Detroit. If so, this seems prescient given the economic transformations that took place over subsequent decades, culminating in the becoming-hegemonic of the creative class and cultural economy alongside a process of deindustrialization and internationalization of production.

3   Bryan-Wilson, Julia (2009) *Art Workers: Radical Practice in the Vietnam War Era*. Berkeley: University of California Press, 45

4   For a consideration of new forms of informal control in cultural labor, see Ross (2003) and Fleming (2009).

5   For more on the history of radical and labor politics in the area, see Forman (1989), Ashley (2012), and Fishman (2005). For a longer history of work itself, see Komlosy (2018).

6   The work taking place in and around Brick Lane also makes evident a different kind of connection to a different kind of factory worker. As stalls run by artists selling self-made artifacts in London are replaced by those selling run-of-the-mill, factory produced garments, trinkets, and souvenirs destined for purchase by tourists visiting the spot on their trips through London, we are reminded of the outsourced workers making these very trinkets in offshore factories in India and China; of the ever-progressing outsourcing and the changing global labor supply

chains (which Ursula Huws writes about); of the new International Division of Cultural Labor (often discussed by the likes of Toby Miller et al.); and of the swathes of offshore-based digital laborers now making up the majority of workers providing, and creating the means of production for, the growing field of digital – but also cultural and artistic – labor.

7   Materials for this chapter were generated primarily through conducting a series of interviews with cultural workers operating in the area around Brick Lane in East London.

8   Gregg, Melissa (2011) *Work's Intimacy*. Cambridge: Polity.

9   Hardt, Michael and Antonio Negri (2009) Commonwealth. Cambridge: Harvard University Press, 250.

10 Banks, Mark (2007) *The Politics of Cultural Work*. Basingstoke: Palgrave, 3.

11 Ibid., 55.

12 McRobbie, Angela (2002) "Clubs to Companies: Notes on the Decline of Political Culture in Speeded Up Creative Worlds." *Cultural Studies* 16, no. 4: 516–31.

13 On this, see van Heur (2010) and Gill and Pratt (2008).

14 On this, see Dowling, Nunes, and Trott (2007); Gorz (2010); Moulier-Boutang (2012); and Lazzarato (1996)

15 Harvey, David (2012) *Rebel Cities: From the Right to the City to the Urban Revolution*. New York: Verso, 139.

16 For more on this, see Florida (2005); Pasquinelli (2008); and Scholz and Liu (2011).

17 Scott, Allen J. (2008) *Social Economy of the Metropolis: Cognitive-Cultural Capitalism and the Global Resurgence of Cities*. Oxford: Oxford University Press, 12-23. These ideas are developed further across Scott's work (1990, 2000).

18 Hardt, Michael, and Antonio Negri (2000) *Empire*. Cambridge: Harvard University Press, 294.

19 On this, see Pink (2010); Gauntlett (2010); Florida (2005); and Arvidsson (2006).

20 On this, see Moulier-Boutang (2012) and Vercellone (2007).

21 Berardi, Franco (2009) *Precarious Rhapsody: Semiocapitalism and the Pathologies of Post-Alpha Generation*. London: Minor Compositions.

22 Dean, Jodi (2009) *Democracy and Other Neoliberal Fantasies: Communicative Capitalism and Left Politics*. Durham: Duke University Press.

23 Fleming, Peter, and Carl Cederström (2012) *Dead Man Working*. Winchester: Zero Books.

24 Lucas, Rob (2010) "Sleep-Worker's Enquiry." *EndNotes*, no. 2: 154–66.

25 "The good worker sleeps well – for the simple man who has completed his labors by the book, this represents a greater reward than his salary; the victims of insomnia are the others – the slackers, the idle, and the indolent." Laurent de Sutter, (2017: 47) *Narcocapitalism: Life in the Age of Anaesthesia*.

26 Haider, Asad, and Salar Mohandesi (2013) "Workers' Inquiry: A Genealogy." *Viewpoint Magazine*, no. 3. viewpointmag.com/2013/09/27/workers-inquiry-a-genealogy.

27 Wright, Steve (2003) *Storming Heaven: Class Composition and Struggle in Italian Autonomist Marxism*. London: Pluto.

28 Figiel, Joanna, Stevphen Shukaitis, and Abe Walker, Eds. (2014) "The Politics of Workers' Inquiry." *ephemera: theory and politics in organization* 14, no. 3: http://www.ephemerajournal.org/issue/politics-workers-inquiry

29 For a critical analysis of entrepreneurship, see Jones and Spicer (2009) and Bill (2006).
30 Fleming, Peter (2009) *Authenticity and the Cultural Politics of Work: New Forms of Informal Control*. Oxford: Oxford University Press.
31 Neff, Gina, Elizabeth Wissinger, and Sharon Zukin (2005) "Entrepreneurial Labor among Cultural Producers: 'Cool' Jobs in 'Hot' Industries." *Social Semiotics* 15, no. 3: 308–33.
32 Ross, Andrew (2009) *Nice Work If You Can Get It: Life and Labor in Precarious Times*. New York: New York University Press, 75.
33 Negrey, Cynthia (2012) *Work Time: Conflict, Control and Change*. Cambridge: Polity, 94.
34 McRobbie, Angela (2002) "Clubs to Companies: Notes on the Decline of Political Culture in Speeded Up Creative Worlds." *Cultural Studies* 16, no. 4, 518.
35 Foucault, Michel (2008) *The Birth of Biopolitics: Lectures at the Collège de France, 1978-1979*. New York: Palgrave Macmillan, 226.
36 Raqs Media Collective (2009) "How to be an artist at night." In *Art school: (propositions for the 21st century*. Ed. Steven Henry Madoff. Cambridge: MIT Press, 71.
37 Hall, Stuart (2003) "New Labour's Double-Shuffle." *Soundings*, no. 24, 17.
38 Read, Jason (2009) "A Genealogy of Homo-Economicus: Neoliberalism and the Production of Subjectivity." *Foucault Studies* Number 6: 25–36.
39 For more on this, see Binkley (2014) and Dardot and Laval (2013).
40 Ross, Andrew (2009), 75.
41 Forkert, Kirsten (2013) *Artistic Lives: A Study of Creativity in Two European Cities*. Farnham: Ashgate.
42 Neff, Gina, Elizabeth Wissinger, and Sharon Zukin (2005), 331.

43 Antunes, Ricardo (2012) *The Meanings of Work: Essay on the Affirmation and Negation of Work*. Leiden: Brill, 104.

44 Gielen, Pascal (2009) *The Murmuring of the Artistic Multitude: Global Art, Memory and Post-Fordism*. Amsterdam: Valiz.

45 Roggero, Gigi (2011) *The Production of Living Knowledge: The Crisis of the University and the Transformation of Labor in Europe and North America*. Philadelphia: Temple University Press, 23.

Knows No Weekend

The aesthetic force of production is the same as that of productive labor and has the same teleology; and what may be called aesthetic relations of production-all that in which the productive force is embedded and in which it is active-are sedimentations or imprintings of social relations of production. Art's double character as both autonomous and fait social is incessantly reproduced on the level of its autonomy. – Theodor Adorno[1]

> Depending on your point of view, either this reformulation of the psychological contract licenses a re-engineering of human personality to suit the ends of the corporation, or the company is simply taking on the roles of other declining social institutions by meeting employees' need for purpose, identification and personal affirmation. – Madeline Bunting[2]

In 1971, the curator and gallerist Rene Block asked Joseph Beuys to produce something for an ongoing series of prints and portfolio he was assembling entitled "Weekend." Beuys is said to have responded to this request with the comment, "Ich kenne kein Weekend," or, "I know no weekend." But rather than just giving a flippant reply, Beuys then proceeded to produce a piece for a series with that very name, one which was compromised of a Maggi sauce bottle and a copy of Immanuel Kant's *Critique of Pure Reason* emblazoned with the text "BEUYS – Ich Kenne Kein Weekend," mounted inside a suitcase along with a series of other prints. In subsequent years, Beuys made a series of lithograph prints using the same text. And in 2014, Rene Block chose Beuys's response as the title for the exhibition marking the 50th anniversary of his Berlin gallery.

While Beuys's initial reply might seem like a pithy come back to an invitation that he may or may not have appreciated, it did indeed hit upon a truth that resonates more deeply than it might appear at first. Whether one believes in the possibility of exercising pure reason in the fashion Kant thought it possible, in his response Beuys expresses something that has become much more commonly realized and analyzed today, namely the apparent impossibility for those engaged in artistic and cultural work to find an outside to their labor. As an artist, Beuys is best known for formulating his artistic practice as participatory and democratic, which he referred to as 'social sculpture,' and for his argument that 'everyone is an artist.' In the workings of today's cultural and creative economy, ever-larger sections of the population are engaged in activities that have been characterized as demonstrating their position in the creative class, or as part of a broader transformation of the economy where forms immaterial and cultural production occupy an increasingly central role.

This chapter explores a somewhat different, and a more specific, focus – that is, to begin to develop an analysis starting from Beuys' statement and reflections emerging from our Metropolitan Factory project. To take seriously the claim that Beuys makes, that it is not possible for him to know a weekend, to know an outside of work, would mean that for those engaged in artistic and cultural work there is also a transformed relationship to work itself. What Beuys gestures to in that claim is the suggestion that artistic forms of labor transform the psychological contract of work, or the informal expectations and norms around the meaning and practices of working.

Denise Rousseau defines the psychological contract as the nature of expected duties and obligations around work, which are not just formally specified within contracts but embedded in a whole range of cultural norms and understanding about work. Rousseau differentiates the psychological contract as the relationship between an individual and a particular organization, and the expectations and norms involved in that employment relationship, from the social contract of work, which she describes as being "cultural, based on shared collective beliefs regarding appropriate behavior in a society."³ While there is some methodological sense in this distinction, when looking at the 'traditional' and relatively stable employment relationship between an individual and a formal and generally stable organization, this becomes blurrier in the workings of dispersed networks of collaboration that characterize freelance cultural workers. In this sense, the psychological contract of work always connects to the social contract of work, and thus here we tend to blur the distinctions between them.

For Beuys, to be an artist is to make peace with the reality that there can be no outside to one's work, that every moment could be seized upon as a space of production, and thus there could be no space of respite from work, no weekend retreat. Pascal Gielen, in his book *The Murmuring of the Artistic Multitude*, argues that the modern art world has played a central role in the movement of ideas of creativity, innovation, flexibility into workings of the economy and labor markets: "the social structure of the early modern art world was one of the social laboratories in which the current Post-Fordian work ethic was produced."⁴ That is to say, this idea that Beuys succinctly expressed of having no outside to work, was first developed within the social laboratory of artistic practice, but arguably has now become more generalized as a model of working and relationship with work.

If the condition that Beuys describes was one freely embraced by artists as a mode of integrating work and life into an overall mode of living and way of being in the world, since then it has shifted to something more generalized, and arguably more pernicious. This 'knows no weekend' formulation of integrating life and work forms of the basis of what Sharon Zukin theorizes as the 'artistic mode of production,'[5] where the lifestyle of artists and their efforts to integrate work and life form a kind of psychological template that the middle classes want to emulate in their living conditions. And it is this idea, this perception of the Bohemian lifestyle, which has fueled the development and gentrification of cities starting with Manhattan and then replicated countless times around the world. The irony is that while the norm of having a high emotional and psychological investment in one's work has become a much more prevalent expectation, it has been accompanied by a much greater degree of uncertainty and stability in working conditions: the becoming-precarious of increasingly vast swathes of formerly secure and permanent forms of employment. It is part of what Martijn Konings describes as the emotional logic of capitalism,[6] one which far from eroding attachments rather tends to foster new ones. It is these attachments that structure the ways in which the future is conceived, always tying it back to work, but less of any sense of security around it. Or as Melissa Gregg describes it, the condition experienced by workers today "is to be invested in work as and when required but without the reciprocal assurance from employers that commitment will be rewarded. Such a scenario risks losing the goodwill of employees permanently."[7] In other words, today it is increasingly common to expect that people will work like artists in the sense Beuys describes, but with ever diminishing guarantees that the high degree of their commitment to work will be rewarded in any way.

Maurizio Lazzarato has argued that the dynamics of the new economy, with higher subjective investment in forms of symbolic, creative, and immaterial labor, has "all been absorbed by the debt economy."[8] Following Ned Rossiter, we could say that it has been likewise absorbed and mitigated by the dynamics of the logistical economy and its nightmares. The question then is what directs and organizes the interface between the highly subjective mode of labor management through the high investment of psychological and libidinal energies, and the more dispersed logistical arrays of capture and governance. Or as Rossiter puts it, if "infrastructure makes worlds, then software coordinates them,"[9] which is exactly why developing a media theory of logistics is a pressing task. It is, however, still important when developing this more structural level analysis to not let go of the insights from autonomist analysis that focus on the composition and subjectivity of living labor, and its potentials for disruptive and system changing resistance and rebellion.[10] The violence of logistics might very well have arisen precisely to attempt to contain these potentials, but is never entirely successful. The expanded psychological contract of cultural production is a system update for the software of the neoliberal governance of labor, one that is constantly attempting to reformat and restrict imaginations of the future to be amenable to the needs of financialization.

Work Without Guarantees

> America, one of the world's richest countries, has decided that the social pact between employer and employee is no longer relevant. There are no guarantees. The party is over. The crashing thud of expectations and hopes have come tumbling down like a decrepit building caught in a strong wind.
> – Jeff Kelly[11]

The sociologist John Clammer has suggested that it would be desirable to develop not just a new sociology of art, but rather what he describes as a "sociology from art," taking moments of artistic and cultural production as containing within themselves understandings, perceptions, and modes of organization that can be teased out into more developed sociological understanding.[12] Arguably this statement from Joseph Beuys points to one such possibility for exploring how an expansive and all-embracing relationship to work that is often found by artists and cultural workers, who frequently demonstrate their commitment to their particular practice above all else, can then become generalized as a model of working: a new psychological contract of labor for precarious times.

There is a range of different sociological and theoretical traditions analyzing the changing nature of work, labor more generally, and the employment relationship. In recent years, there have been increased efforts to find bridges between some of them and the analysis of arts and cultural production.[13] These discussions find parallels in the art world in the emergence of institutional critique during the 1960s and 1970s, which develops out of social movement organizing and radical politics as a space where artists can discuss and contest the nature of power and authority in the institutions in which they operate, namely galleries and museums. It is interesting, and perhaps somewhat ironic, that despite the focus being on the operations of such institutions, the focus tended to be more on questions of the connections between museums of the military industrial complex, racism, and discrimination in the art world, and less on the concrete working conditions of artists.[14] This is of course not to claim that questions about race, gender, and sexuality are not important by any means. Rather than anything, it seems to reinforce what Hans Abbing argues,[15] that artists have an ideological and psychological investment in thinking about their labors as something other than work, something other and exceptional to everyday concerns, which makes it unnerving to talk about one's practice in the same way you might discuss any other form of work. But increasing conditions of precarity and uncertainty, which have become generalized after the dismantling of the Fordist-Keynesian state welfare model, have rendered attempts to continue viewing artistic and cultural work as exceptional to other labor as unviable.

As Hito Steyerl has suggested, if the first wave of institutional critique produced integration into the art institutions, and the second wave worked to achieve representation into those institutions, since then the only integration to achieve has been into precarious working conditions. Steyerl suggests that institutional critique has now been weaponized by neoliberal politics, where concerns previously expressed about the nature of power and authority in cultural institutions is now used as a pretext for dismantling of those very institutions:

> while critical institutions are being dismantled by neoliberal institutional

criticism, this produces an ambivalent subject which develops multiple strategies for dealing with its dislocation. It is on the one side being adapted to the needs of ever more precarious living conditions. On the other, the need seems never to have been greater for institutions that could cater to the new needs and desires that this constituency will create.[16]

This weaponizing of critique develops, perhaps much in the same way that it has been argued, that the 'new spirit of capitalism' transformed discontent with Fordist labor practices into a justification for more flexible forms of alienation and exploitation. This becomes distilled down into pop managerial versions by people like Daniel Pink who claim that carrots and sticks, or traditional forms of rewards and discipline, have become outmoded for today's world of work, which instead requires an embracing of the principles of autonomy, mastery, and purpose.[17] Arguably it is a desire for the ability to work in a self-directed fashion, to be able to be one's own boss, that motivates both those pursuing particular forms of artistic and cultural practice, and entrepreneurs.

This is what Steyerl gestures to as the ambivalent subject who is dislocated. The initial motivating drives have become generalized as a form of ubiquitous labor discipline, one that is all the more effective precisely because it operates through a dispersed and self-organized form of imposition. Artistic and cultural workers, rather than finding themselves confronted by a boss or a manager issuing orders and disciplining their work, find themselves confronting *themselves* finding ever more complex ways to squeeze time and energy out of their own creative work, but also other paid 'gigs,' jobs, and often other – sometimes unpaid commitments required to keep them afloat. While Beuys might have known no weekend as a freely embraced choice, for precarious artistic and cultural workers today trying to make ends meet, it can become rather difficult to make any other choice. Directly confronting or questioning this logic is all the more difficult precisely because of the deep-seated psychological investment in the work, in a form of artistic and cultural practice, which can easily end up being as much about forming a psychological sense of identity as being a form of labor.

Marx On Silkworms &
the labor of the Self

> a new discourse about work, one that might be termed the search for 'pleasure in work,' to distinguish it from that slogan of infamous memory, 'joy through work'... it is the outcome of a series of reforms and experiments conceived in response to a malaise caused by the pursuit of productivity... measures are intended to make work come to be perceived not just as a matter of pure constraint but as a good in itself: as a means towards self-realization rather than as an opportunity for self-transcendence. – Jacques Donzelot[18]

One productive avenue for exploring this deep-seated psychological investment in work can be found in a suggestive argument that Marx makes in exploring the difference between productive and unproductive work, or more specifically between work that is productive for capital versus that which is not. To make this distinction he brings up rather curiously the figure of John Milton, the author of *Paradise Lost*, a celebrated piece of literature which is widely regarded as one of the best-known epic poems. But as Marx points out, from the perspective of capital and value production, Milton is far from being a productive worker. How is that so? Simply because Milton engaged with an epic amount of labor, most likely taking years, in order to produce this literary work, which he then sold on for publishing. The amount of work involved is hugely disproportionate to the value created, at least in the short term, for capital. This can be distinguished from the hack journalist who appears to only engage in writing specifically because that writing is useful as a saleable commodity, not for any intrinsic worth found within.

This for Marx is the key distinction. Milton's labor is of value not because it produces value for capital, but in the sense that it is a labor of the self, it is a labor that expressed something close to Milton's own nature:

> Milton produced *Paradise Lost* in the way that a silkworm produces silk, as the expression of his own nature... the Leipzig literary proletarian who produces books... at the instructions of his publisher is roughly speaking a productive worker, in so far as

his production is subsumed under capital and only takes place for the purpose of the latter's valorization.[19]

Here is the key difference. Milton's labor in writing is not producing value for capital, but is only value producing when it enters into circuits of commodity production and exchange. Marx extends this analysis following with the image that a singer who sings like a bird is an unproductive worker, but once she sells that capacity to sing as a form of labor power, then she produces directly produces capital. This is a clear statement of the well-known distinction Marx makes that value for capital is only produced by labor enmeshed in circuits of commodity production and exchange, which has been debated and disputed.

What is more interesting than the productive and unproductive distinction is what Marx attributes to Milton's labor before it becomes enmeshed in circuits of commodity production. For Marx, this labor that is unproductive for capital is like the silkworm producing silk, which is to say that it is not motivated by the prospect of external reward, but because it is an intrinsic part of the silkworm's nature. The work of the silkworm is an expression of its intrinsic nature, rather than something developed or motivated by external reward. If the silkworm were a cultural worker, it would probably tell Marx, or us, that it is only concerned about developing its own practice rather than commercial concerns.

In the context of changing psychological contracts around cultural work, there is a clear drive to transform increasing parts of work, so that they are experienced by the worker as the expression of the worker's own nature – much like a silkworm producing silk. If work is experienced or perceived as flowing directly from one's own creative nature, then it is not, more often than not, even recognized as work. This is the idea that underpins the entire celebrated mantra of 'doing what you love' as a way to escape the drudgery of work and routine into conditions, in which work and play blend into a winning situation of turning one's passion into an activity that one can live off of, at least in theory.[20] Here, psychological contracts operate as a form of normative control, giving workers the impression that there is a reciprocal bargain that the employer or client will live up to (without any necessary guarantee that this will be the case). Or, as John Budd frames it, the "true power of psychological contracts... might be in making a hierarchical employment relationship seem balanced to employees and thereby providing legitimacy for the existing social order."[21]

There seems to be an ideological celebration of work that is part of one's own nature. The problem with this is that such celebration does not mean that such work magically becomes a viable means of supporting oneself. Rather, there is a value in this idea, despite that it is far from a realistic option for many people. Here can be seen an example of what Jason Read, following Foucault, describes as neoliberalism's formatting of subjectivity, its demands that we are to be entrepreneurs of ourselves.[22] Neoliberalism in this view is not just about changing conditions of regulation or governance of social structure, but about producing certain kinds of social relationships, in particular the shaping of subjective experiences of self in relationship with work, encouraging people to view themselves as human capital.

In this way, we can connect Beuys' claim that everyone is an artist with Marx's description of Milton's labor being of his own nature. By developing perceptions of certain forms of work as being of intrinsic value, as producing our own nature, we can draw a connection to understanding work as a form of human capital creation. In this way authentic forms of labor, as expressions of the self, come to function as a form of regulating and intensifying work. This can be seen not just within the importance often held by artists and cultural workers to seek out meaningful work, but also in how notions of authentic expression and meaningful work become adopted as corporate policies. Or as Peter Fleming has put it, the guiding motto for workers becomes to 'just be themselves,' but this is no longer a choice but a requirement, and a new form of informal control that operates through the appearance of its informality and desirability.[23]

Who would not want to work in an environment where work is meaningful, where you can be yourself? At face value, it is difficult to even argue against such notions that present themselves as inherently positive and unproblematic without a good degree of unpacking their contradictions and hidden forms of discipline. But what does it mean when wanting to engage in forms of authentic and meaningful work have shifted into a form of labor discipline? This is especially the case when the motivating desire to finding authenticity and meaning in work becomes part of leading one into accepting precarious conditions or arrangements. Precarity is thus not just about the formal job status, but also regulating the production of subjectivity in relationship with work itself. It is part of producing what Fleming calls the 'I, job' function, or where our very sociality is now deeply implicated as part of the production process.[24]

Social Reproduction & the Underpinning of Cultural Work

> The primary characteristic of self-employment is the *domestication* of the workplace, the assimilation of work within the rules of private life, even when the two spaces – home and work – are kept separate… The workplace simply established by the independent worker, such that the culture and habits of one's private life are transferred to the workplace. – Sergio Bologna[25]

Reflecting on matters of social reproduction, we see similarities between embodied artistic and creative labor to gendered instances of reproductive labor. If work is seen as part of oneself – in this sense, highly invested, embodied creative work, work that becomes one's life and *vice versa* – it is similar to various instances of gendered, feminized types of labor that are involved in processes of daily social production and reproduction, care work, and housework. Similarly, this kind of work, artistic and feminized labor, is dependent on the wider social networks of informal and flexible support and assistance. In the past, the feminized work of social reproduction in the home would have depended on the single wage of a Fordist worker (male) while it simultaneously *made his work possible* and sustainable in the first place. In the current climate of increasing precarity, artistic and creative work depends increasingly on family money, inherited property, as well as parental, sibling or spousal income and support. This artistic and creative production is also dependent on extra-familial, less formalized means of support such as mutual childcare provision, vegetable coops, and skills exchanges.

Even highly autonomous and individualized workers who perhaps stay away, consciously, from collaborative ways of working and value production rely on such relationships and collaborations in order to be able to survive and continue with their creative practices. These types of artistic work could be looked at from the perspective of 1970s feminist work, Wages for Housework and Silvia Federici's ideas.[26] Further, instances of unpaid work, labor of self-investment and nurturing social connections, networking and so on – not necessarily just in the creative sector or in the arts,[27] although here the similarity to feminized work in the home is more obvious – in order to be considered as work, can be thought about in the way Wages for Housework thought of labor of social production and reproduction or housework in the home. In order to discuss such activities in terms of *work*, a demand for a wage, needed to be made in order to refuse such work.

Many of the cultural producers who are being pushed out from newly gentrified areas cannot afford a separate studio space or paid access to a co-working space, and so they take their work back into the home, or indeed, it has never left the domestic setting in the first place. This is of course, in a sense – ironically – correspondent to the trajectory of types of art and craft work that was initially predominantly feminized work and only left the home and entered the sphere of value production at the time of the industrial revolution (alongside the work of children and women) only to return to the sphere of the domestic yet again. This overlap between domestic work and unpaid work clearly affects both the working and domestic situation – looking after the kids or further relying on family for help with work and or accommodations, the strain this type of work has on relationships, etc. – this being generally the caring and affective labor performed by women, it further affects this category of workers.

Precarity as the Governance of Cultural labor

> The real structures of social reproduction and domination present themselves in a personalized; namely, as a system of personal relations of dependence and obligation
> – Robert Kurz[28]

> the social precariousness of employment is not just a matter of occupational

insecurity and labor market uncertainty, but is shaped by the mismatch between the official imagination of work and significations derived from its ordinary material experiences. – Franco Barchiesi[29]

Shifts in the psychological and social contract of cultural labor are thus part of this formatting of subjectivity as demanded and required by neoliberalism. This operates most effectively when the deep investment required in the work itself presents itself not as a burden or a risk, but rather as something desirable and enjoyable. Gina Neff, Elizabeth Wissinger, and Sharon Zukin describe how this can be seen in "how entrepreneurial labor becomes intertwined with work identities in cultural industries both on and off the job" for media and cultural workers.[30] Workers are drawn into and find working in these industries desirable because of the cool factor associated with them, as well as the allure of work that is thought to have a high degree of autonomy, creativity, and excitement, and thus came to accept the risks that are also associated with such forms of work, to know no weekends. Going to a party after work is no longer just going to a party, but also an occasion for compulsory networking, for meeting the requirements of being seen at the right place at the right time to maintain a certain image required for work.

A great amount of time and work, or rather, entrepreneurial labor is spent on networking, maintaining both closer and more distant contacts and relationships with people in the industry in order to provide the next job, the next gig, or even just to remain visible in the field. This is of course all unpaid labor, but labor that can be seen as part of being an entrepreneur of the self, a work, or investing, or perhaps speculating on one's human capital.[31] This kind of entrepreneurship, or 'social self-investment' can be seen in unpaid internships in the creative and cultural sector.[32] Just as there are now many similarities between the artistic and cultural mode of production and other spheres of the post-Fordist and now highly precarious economy, there are similarities between the kinds of unpaid labor required on the part of recent graduates and interns, and the unpaid, invisible labor of artistic and cultural workers struggling to stay afloat in the weekend-less, precarious economy.

Neff has explored further how this dynamic of psychological and social self-investment does not confine itself to occupations more obviously thought of as artistic and cultural, but is embraced more widely across tech and media sectors. She describes this phenomenon as venture labor, or the "investment of time, energy, human capital, and other personal resources that ordinary employees make in the companies they work. Venture labor is the explicit expression of entrepreneurial values by non-entrepreneurs."[33] What Neff calls venture labor is a space where the expanded and transformed psychological contract of work that was seen in the arts is expanded into other areas. Venture labor for Neff describes how workers are convinced to take on risks and apply themselves harder to their work because they perceive these actions as having the character of future investment in better outcomes which may not be monetary at all, but are rather more related to the success of the firm or the project. In other words, even if they do not explicitly think about it in such terms, the venture laborer has become willing to apply themselves to their work much like Milton as silkworm, as engaging in a labor of their own nature, which they are committed, more for the intrinsic reward of it than economic benefit. But the key difference here is that this does not mean that the tech workers Neff describes actually have ownership or formally invest in the company. Venture labor describes their willingness to work as if they did, out of their psychological and social investment in the work, despite that not being the case. Through this intensified psychological investment in work, the imagination of the future becomes financialized. It is subject to the continued demands of capital's continued valorization, its expected return on investments. Except these workers are not even themselves directly as financialized as much as this relationship, governing the imagination of the future, is culturally mediated through their relationship with work.

It could be argued that these kinds of venture labor appropriate and reproduce the mechanisms of gendered unpaid reproductive and domestic labor, specifically, the invisible care and maintenance that workers perform both on themselves and for the organizations they work for. Rather than acknowledge these activities as exploitative forms of unpaid labor however, they are often presented as necessary (even desirable) investments, both for the artistic and cultural worker – and beyond, as well as more generally for a functioning, productive, profitable society. Angela Mitropoulos argues the neoliberalism and post-Fordism represent a complex rewriting and transformation of the social contracts underlying conceptions of the family, sexuality and social reproduction, which is co-articulated through overlapping dynamics of gender, race, citizenship, and borders. It is not surprising that this affects the workings of cultural production as well.[34]

Venture labor operates as an effective form of governing forms of labor that are less amenable to more traditional workplace discipline precisely for how it encourages workers to embrace economic risk, but without any guarantee of reward or security. Neff argues that embrace of risk, in individualized form, "does not bode well for organizing collective, social responses to support work in innovative industries."[35] This echoes arguments previously made by Angela McRobbie about how cultural and media workers are expected to operate as 'microstructures,' taking on all the tasks associated within managerial labor, but to absorb them into their own work.[36] In both cases, it is suggested that this embrace of risk, the shift of the psychological and social contract of work, operate to effectively block off what previously had the possibility of acting as a starting point for collective organizing around a form of work. Both of these dynamics function as part of what Franco 'Bifo' Berardi describes as the slow cancellation of the future which began during the 1970s and 1980s, emerging with the rise of neoliberalism.[37] Likewise, Mark Fisher describes how this erosion of the future, and of the imagination of possible futures, has served to deflate expectations of what can be accomplished through collective organizing.[38]

It is in this sense of blocking off or pre-empting labor organizing, which is to say functioning as a form of governing labor, that the transformed psychological and social contract of work connects with the question of precarious labor and conditions. This can be clearly seen in Guy Standing's work on the emergence of the precariat as a distinctive class, in which he argues that the precariat has distinct class characteristics based on having minimal trust relationships with capital or the state, which is to say with the organizational forms that have previously governed the employment relationship. Standing argues that precarious workers today no longer have or can fall back on the social contract relied upon by the proletariat during Fordism, namely where "labor securities were provided in exchange for subordination and contingent loyalty, the unwritten deal underpinning welfare states."[39] Standing argues that the class position of precarious workers is unique precisely because of this shift in expectations, the lack of a bargain of security for subordination, which previously existed. Instead, workers are faced with, as argued by Melissa Gregg, with an expectation of high investment and commitment in their work, but with no guarantee of any security. Standing suggests that precarious workers have a truncated status, one that does not map easily onto high status professional or middle class occupations, even if it is held together by the psychological and social celebration of these forms of work as meaningful and rewarding.

This truncated status easily becomes a continual source of uncertainty due to the mismatch between expectations and realities. Work is supposed to be highly rewarding and fulfilling, characterized by creativity and self-organization, yet that is more often than not coupled with uncertainty about whether contracts will be continued, whether new projects will pan out, what conditions can be expected tomorrow. For these reasons, it perhaps no surprise at all that it would be claimed, as it has been by the Institute for Precarious Consciousness, that the dominant affective structure is precisely one of anxiety.[40] The Fordist production line and the welfare state might have brought about conditions of a more secure survival, though often argued by dissidents from the Situationists to the Sex Pistols, to be paired with misery and boredom. Today we no longer struggle to escape from the boredom of predictability and security, but rather worry and are anxious about loss of status, subsistence, or other conditions. Precarious cultural and artistic workers discover that their freedom and autonomy is purchased at the price of buying into what Franco 'Bifo' Berardi describes as the psychopathologies of immaterial and informational work, the way that it overloads abilities to process and communicate.[41]

In this way, the conditions of precarious work fundamentally alter the relationship between wage and income, as payments received for temporary work (particularly within the arts and cultural sector) are often not enough to support one's existence. If temporary work cannot be relied upon for supporting material sustenance, even while it is being relied upon as a form of psychological wage or sustenance of sense of identity and meaning, then it becomes necessary to find all kinds of means and strategies to make ends meet. Monthly budgets are precariously balanced on managing credit debts, leading to what Randy Martin described aptly as the financialization of daily life, as well as conceptions of the future that emerge from these everydays.[42] This may take the form of taking up additional work unrelated to one's practice in order to support working in the arts and culture sector, or finding other means of support, or constantly developing other skills and capacities that may become useful in obtaining future work and/or support for one's artistic-cultural practice. And it is by this acting as entrepreneurs of self-demanded by the neoliberal formatting of subjectivity where workers develop

> across their lifetime, in the workplace and at home, behavioral, communicative, and cognitive skills needed to face employment risks, compete in uncertain labor markets, and cope with frequent jobs changes. To the extent that workers acquire such capacities outside the conventionally

defined working hours, employers can appropriate them at no cost[43]

But why would workers be willing to acquire new skills and capacities outside working hours if such are going to be freely appropriated at no cost? Again, here it can be seen how the expanded psychological and social contract of work operates, where doing that extra labor of self-development can be justified it can be seen to be part of supporting and making possible one's form of artistic or cultural practice. Beyond the relatively narrow area of artistic and cultural work it is the upskilling demanded that today's venture laborers must continually participate in, in order to demonstrate their continued investment in working conditions that continue not to guarantee them any security, but rather continue to demand ongoing displays of this deep-seated investment in work without any guarantees.

This is what Isabell Lorey described as when precarity becomes a form of governmentalization. That is, when precarious conditions are not just about changing the conditions of work, or the withdrawal of regulations or protections that once existed, but seek to actively change the ways in which subjectivity is formed. For Lorey, this governmental precarization is not only about changing the conditions of employment, but also the "destabilization of the conduct of life and thus of bodies and modes of subjectivation."[44] And most importantly, this transformation in subjectiviation through becoming precarious for Lorey is no longer a marginal phenomenon, but indeed have arrived at what she describes as the 'social middle' where "[p]recarious living and working conditions are increasingly normalized at a structural level… the society we currently live in is by no means an insecurity society, it is indeed still a security society, but it is one that can be controlled through social insecurity."[45] Here, Beuys' embrace of knowing no weekend shifts from enabling a new possibility for his work, to functioning as a kind of model of governing labor.

Ambivalence & Passion

> We have to face up to the fact that there is no automatically available road to resistance and organization for artistic labor. That opportunism and competition are not a

deviation of this form of labor but its inherent structure. That this workforce is not ever going to march in unison, except perhaps while dancing to a viral Lady Gaga imitation video. The international is over. Now let's get on with the global. – Hito Steyerl[46]

After reading thus far, where does this leave questions about the nature of cultural and artistic labor, if indeed our relationship to it has changed through an expansion of the psychological and social contract of work? If we are, or were, attracted to working in the words of artistic and cultural production because of their formation around what Angela McRobbie calls "passionate work,"[47] what can be done when it is precisely that passionate attachment to work that serves to facilitate and make possible conditions of even more intense exploitation, that makes bearable forms of precarity that would otherwise be rejected? What are you willing to accept in order to sustain the burden of your passion? Is it necessary to jettison the entire idea of meaningful and fulfilling work because of this, and if so, in favor of what?

We would suggest that is not the case. As gestured to in the quote from Hito Steyerl above, there is no automatically available approach for the organizing of artistic and cultural labor, including a wholesale rejection of passionate motivation and attachment to the work itself. Rather, it is a question of working through ambivalent genealogies of precarious work, creativity, and motivation that have led us to the present. And working through them not to discard them, but rather to reclaim the utopian potentials that can still be found within the condition of the realization of Beuys' claim that everyone is an artist. How can we become creators not just of exploitable forms of creativity, but of other ways of producing and live together? How is it possible to refuse work from a position of a precarious worker, who only ever had an intermittent, unfulfilling, temporary and/or underpaid relationship to the very work that also defines her subjectivity and psychologically? As Kathi Weeks suggests, many of the numerous problems with work today are tied to the hegemony of the work ethic, which today "is even more central because in forms of post-Fordist production there is an enormous need for workers willing to invest their subjectivity and to identify with their work."[48]

In Italy during the rise of autonomist movement in the late 1970s it was proclaimed that precarity was a beautiful thing. This beauty was celebrated because it was an escape from the controls of boredom of the Fordist factory line into something new and unexpected, attempts to find new ways to live through self-organized forms of work, living, and cultural activity.[49] Of course, this embrace of precarity and uncertainty would no longer have the same appeal, present itself with the same beauty, once the rollback of the welfare state and the undermining of other forms of material and psychological security meant that precarity was no longer a choice to be embraced by those who desired it but a condition to be endured by all. And it is in this sense that precarious labor and our investments in it, whether in cultural and artistic work, is ambivalent. Gigi Roggero argues that it is ambivalent in a strong sense, as space of conflict that is not dialectical in the more traditional Marxist sense, but rather "a field of antagonistic forces, focusing on the new terrain of conflict and its possibilities outside of every deterministic premise, therefore illustrating its elements of historicity and contingency."[50]

Such is the ambivalence of passionate work: not wanting to let go of it, not wanting to be done with forms of work that drive us so that *not knowing the weekend* might indeed be fully justified. Ambivalence, not as a mere discomfort, but meaning, in a deeper sense, that transformations in labor contain a possibility to go in two very different directions: towards a financialized future desire to capital accumulation, or a struggle towards a future where creativity forms the basis of new horizons for cooperation and solidarity. The problem lies in finding ways to channel this desire into forms of work that are not premised on accepting precarity as its precondition. In other words, it would make no sense to dismiss the desires of cultural workers to find meaning and fulfillment in their work, to tell them that these desires allow them to be exploited and should be done away with. The question of what becomes possible, in terms of reclaiming of a utopian imagination, starting from how these desires are cramped within the spaces afforded within these precarious times. We still want to know weekends, even if they do not fall on Saturdays and Sundays. We must reclaim the utopian dream of a self-organized future rather than succumb to its slow cancellation brought on by neoliberalism and its financialized governance of culture, labor, and life in general. There may indeed be no ready-made road to resistance for artistic and cultural labor, but that does not mean that there is no use in constantly re-inventing new forms of labor solidarity and organizing. To know the weekend again means not falling back into a Faustian bargain that understands creative work as meaningful only when it is all encompassing, and thus becomes a pretence for destroying the very conditions that make such work and creativity possible to begin with.

Notes

1. Adorno, Theodor (1997) *Aesthetic Theory*. London: Continuum, 6.
2. Bunting, Madeline (2005) Willing Slaves: How the Overwork Culture is Ruling Our Lives. London: Harper Perennial, 93.
3. Rousseau, Denise (1995) *Psychological Contracts in Organizations: Understanding Written and Unwritten Agreements*. London: Sage, 13. The concept of the psychological contract could usefully be read in relationship with W.E.B. Du Bois described as the "psychological wage." For more on this, see Roediger (1991).
4. Gielen, Pascal (2009) *The Murmuring of the Artistic Multitude: Global Art, Memory and Post-Fordism*. Amsterdam: Valiz, 2.
5. Zukin, Sharon (1989) *Loft Living: Culture and Capital in Urban Change*. New Brunswick: Rutgers University Press.
6. Konings, Martijn (2015) *The Emotional Logic of Capitalism*. Stanford: Stanford University Press.
7. Gregg, Melissa (2011) *Work's Intimacy*. London: Polity, 165.
8. Lazzarato, Maurizio (2012) *The Making of the Indebted Man*. Los Angeles: Semiotext(e), 8.
9. Rossiter, Ned (2016) *Software, Infrastructure, Labor: A Media Theory of Logistical Nightmares*. New York: Routledge, xv. See also Cowen, Deborah (2014) *The Deadly Life of Logistics*. Minneapolis: University of Minnesota Press.
10. One of the main source for rethinking the role of labor and politics in participatory media that draws heavily on the work of Hardt and Negri as well the traditions of thought that draw from is Tiziana

Terranova's writing on the function of "free labor" within network cultures (2004). Terranova's analysis of free labor as both exploited and enjoyable, and as functioning as a necessary feature of networked forms of immaterial labor, has functioned as a key nodal for in the development of research using autonomist concepts. This connects back to a larger project of class composition analysis, and in particular as a form of worker's inquiry. The notion of worker's inquiry, developed within autonomist movements, was not meant as a way to develop new sociological categories, bur rather to understand the transformations of forms of labor that were occurring from within them, and from that the political possibilities that they contain. In terms of the potential they keep open for antagonistic social analysis, we would locate their usefulness in terms of bringing back to serious consideration a notion of class for conceptualizing media practices, cultural labor, and related dynamics, but a notion of class that is nowhere near as reductive as the more economistic analysis with which Marxism is often associated. Furthermore, an autonomist approach to understanding changes in media and cultural labor emphasizes that forms engagement currently employed by capital to eke out more and more surplus value (e.g., unpaid cultural labor, free labor) are precisely the potential of previous practices that have been rendered into new modes of accumulation (Gielen, 2009; Ross, 2009; Gill and Pratt, 2008; Rossiter and Lovink, 2007). The key point is to understand the ways that a process of class decomposition, turning resistance into new forms of capitalist valorization, occurs such that it can be worked through, around, and against.

11   Kelly, Jeff (1997) *The Best of Temp Slave.* Madison: Garnett County Press.

12   Clammer, John (2014). *Vision and Society: Towards a Sociology and Anthropology from Art.* London: Routledge.

13   For some recent writing and analysis of the shifting relations between art and labor see Aranda, Wood, and Vidokle (2011); Banks (2007); Diederichsen (2008); Klamer (1996) Abbing (2004); Sholette and Ressler (2013); Siebert and Wilson (2013) Siegelbaum (2013); Kálmán and Šević (2010); and Wherry (2012).

14   For more on this, see Raunig and Ray (2009); Fraser (2005); and Alberro and Stimson (2009).

15   Abbing, Hans (2004) *Why Are Artists Poor? The Exceptional Economy of the Arts.* Amsterdam: Amsterdam University Press.

16   Steyerl, Hito (2009) "The Institution of Critique," *Art and Contemporary Critical Practice: Reinventing Institutional Critique.* Gerald Raunig and Gene Ray, Eds. London: MayFly Books, 19.

17   Pink, Daniel (2010) *Drive: The Surprising Truth about What Motivates Us.* Edinburgh: Canongate.

18   Donzelot, Jacques (1991) "Pleasure in work," *The Foucault Effect: Studies in Governmentality.* Ed. Graham Burchell, Colin Gordon, and Peter Miller. Chicago: University of Chicago Press, 251.

19   Marx, Karl (1976) *Capital: Volume 1.* London: Penguin Books, 1044.

20   Tokumitsu, Miya (2015) *Do What You Love: And Other Lies About Success and Happiness.* New York: Regan Arts. This could also usefully be compared with the way that Donzelot on "pleasure in work" (1991). See also Campbell (1989).

21   Budd, John (2011) *The Thought of Work.* Ithaca: Cornell University Press, 114.

22 Read, Jason (2009) "A Genealogy of Homo-Economicus: Neoliberalism and the Production of Subjectivity" *Foucault Studies* Number 6: 25-36.

23 Fleming, Peter (2009) *Authenticity and the Cultural Politics of Work: New Forms of Informal Control*. Oxford: Oxford University Press.

24 Fleming, Peter (2015) *The Mythology of Work: How Capitalism Persists Despite Itself*. London: Pluto Books. But as Gerald Hanlon argues (2015), the involvement of subjective, personal traits, in the work process, could also be argued not to be new, but rather extending dynamics already found within capitalism. A longer term and larger scope analysis of this issue would look not just at it within the working of the cultural economy, but rather as a more fundamental aspect of capitalism itself which, if anything, has become more pronounced rather than being a new development.

25 Bologna, Sergio (2018) *The Rise of the European Self-employed Workforce*. Hythe: Mimesis International, 106.

26 Federici, Silvia (2012) *Revolution at Point Zero: Housework, Reproduction, and Feminist Struggle*. Oakland: PM Press. See also Federici and Austin (2017).

27 And here it could be usefully understood better drawing from the history of feminist art from the period, which was exploring many of the same dynamics. On this, see Wilson (2015).

28 Kurz, Robert (2016) *The Substance of Capital. The Life and Death of Capitalism*. London: Chronos Publications, 16.

29 Barchiesi, Franco (2011) Precarious *Liberation: Workers, the State, and Contested Social Citizenship in Postapartheid South Africa*. Albany: SUNY Press, 24.

30 Neff, Gina, Elizabeth Wissinger, and Sharon Zukin (2005) Entrepreneurial Labor among Cultural Producers: "Cool" Jobs in "Hot" Industries. *Social Semiotics* Volume 15 Number 3, 307.

31 For more on this see Vishmidt, Marina (2018) *Speculation as a Mode of Production: Forms of Value Subjectivity in Art and Capital.* Leiden: Brill.

32 Hope, Sophie and Joanna Figiel (2015) "Interning and Investing: Rethinking Unpaid Work, Social Capital, and the 'Human Capital Regime'," *tripleC* 13(2): 361-374.

33 Neff, Gina (2012) *Venture Labor.* Cambridge: MIT Press, 17.

34 Mitropoulos, Angela (2012) *Contract and Contagion: From Biopolitics to Oikonomia.* New York: Autonomedia.

35 Neff, Gina (2012), 36.

36 McRobbie, Angela (2002) "Clubs to Companies: Notes on the Decline of Political Culture in Speeded Up Creative Worlds," *Cultural Studies* 16, no. 4: 516–31.

37 Berardi, Franco (2011) *After the Future.* Oakland: AK Press.

38 Fisher, Mark (2014) *Ghosts of My Life.* Winchester: Zero Books.

39 Standing, Guy (2011) *The Precariat: The New Dangerous Class.* London: Bloomsbury Academic, 8.

40 nstitute for Precarious Consciousness (2014)

41 Berardi, Franco (2009) *Precarious rhapsody: Semiocapitalism and the pathologies of the post-alpha generation.* London: Minor Compositions.

42 Martin, Randy (2002) *Financialization of Daily Life.* Philadelphia: Temple University Press.

43 Barchiesi, Franco (2011) Precarious *Liberation: Workers, the State, and Contested Social Citizenship in Postapartheid South Africa.* Albany: SUNY Press, 124.

44 Lorey, Isabell (2015) *State of Insecurity: Government of the Precarious.* London: Verso, 13.
45 Lorey, Isabell (2011) "Governmental Precarization," *Transversal* Number 8. Available at http://eipcp.net/transversal/0811/lorey/en
46 Steyerl, Hito (2009) "The Institution of Critique," *Art and Contemporary Critical Practice: Reinventing Institutional Critique.* Gerald Raunig and Gene Ray, Eds. London: MayFly Books, 35.
47 McRobbie, Angela (2016) *Be Creative: Making a Living in the New Culture Industries.* Cambridge: Polity.
48 Curcio, Anna and Weeks, Kathi (2015) "Social Reproduction, Neoliberal Crisis, and the Problem with Work: A Conversation with Kathi Weeks," *Viewpoint* Issue 5. Available at https://viewpointmag.com/2015/10/31/social-reproduction-neoliberal-crisis-and-the-problem-with-work-a-conversation-with-kathi-weeks/
49 Berardi, Franco (2009) *Precarious rhapsody: Semiocapitalism and the pathologies of the post-alpha generation.* London: Minor Compositions.
50 Roggero, Gigi (2011) *The Production of Living Knowledge: The Crisis of the University and the Transformation of Labor in Europe and North America.* Philadelphia: Temple University Press, 21.

Watermelon Politics and the Mutating Forms of Institutional Critique Today

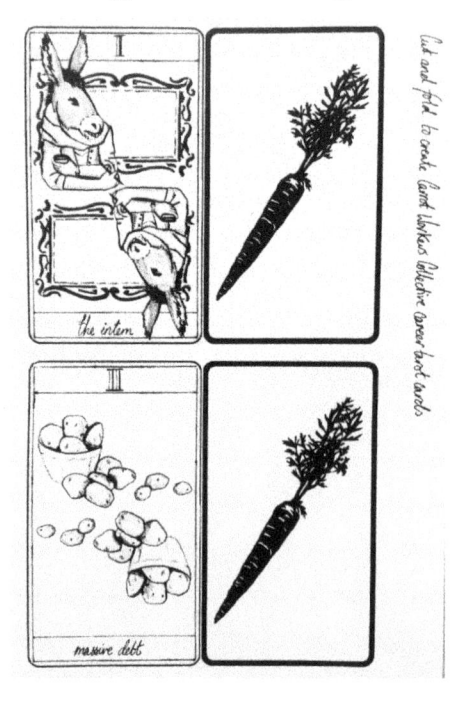

In recent years, there has been a rise of social movements and political formations raising questions about the operations of contemporary art institutions. These have ranged from activist groups such as the Precarious Workers Brigade (PWB)[1] and Working Artists and the Greater Economy (WAGE),[2] among others, questioning the functioning of unpaid labor in the cultural and artistic sector, to Liberate Tate's engagement in ending the relationship of public cultural institutions with oil companies, focused on BP's sponsorship of Tate Modern.[3] While the PWB is actively engaged in the issue of unpaid and often exploitative internships within the arts and cultural sector in the UK, as well as critically examining and deconstructing dominant narratives around work, employability, and careers, WAGE made its mark on the art world by exposing the issue of non-payment of fees for artists working within New York's non-profit arts institutions sector. Given that these groups are acting in response to similar pressures and ethical and political conflicts, they may be seen as direct descendants of those originally engaged in the birth and rise of institutional critique. On the one hand, the fact that similar conditions – despite being recognized as problems for decades

– continue to affect those working in the arts and cultural sector today is a somewhat depressing realization. On the other hand, however, it seems that we are seeing a renewed, and somewhat mutated, institutional critique emerging in new forms today.

In this chapter, we would like to explore the proposition that recent developments in new forms of institutional critique, and their transformations, could be thought to exhibit a kind of watermelon politics, which is to say having an outward concern with issues of ecology and sustainability, but one that also contains – on a deeper level – concerns about issues relating to labor and production. That is to say that doubled, if not trebled, layers of ethical and political concern are central to new forms of activism around art institutions. While the convenient and perhaps somewhat comical metaphor/comparison of a watermelon might give the impression that one layer always concealing another, it is far from it. Rather, we are seeing a different layering and embedding of questions around ethics, labor, sustainability, precarity, and the nature of the institution all working with and often against each other, providing new perspectives and problems for the ongoing question: who runs the art world, and for whose benefit?

Strike Art, or Not

In our view, the best exploration of the most recent flowering of institutional critique is Yates McKee's book, *Strike Art: Contemporary Art and the Post-Occupy Condition.* McKee says he intended it as a "strategic address to those working in the art field more specifically to consider how the various kinds of resources at our disposal might be channeled into movement work as it unfurls with ongoing moments of political rupture."[4] By framing his work in this way, McKee immediately re-opens the question of institutional critique not just within the framework of art history and the art historical canonization critiques of art history, but within a genealogy of moments of political upheaval and contestation. If there would be a renewal of institutional critique today, the reasons for it would not be found within the logic of institutions but rather in the spaces formed by active revolt against them, or what McKee describes succinctly in the subtitle as the 'post-Occupy' conditions. These involve and include, beyond Occupy as a discrete movement or moment, all forms of related political upheaval ranging from the Arab Spring to Black Lives Matter, also drawing from a renewed political grammar of seizing spaces to create moments of encounter where other forms of subjectivity, and thus hopefully other forms of politics, can emerge.

One of the aspects of McKee's work is that while it can be seen how such forms of political contestation are related to the art world, they do not necessarily solely relate to – or remain within – the art world. Instead, their orientation to the art world is just one among many articulations of their existence. This can be seen in the exploration of the Gulf Labor Artist Coalition, which operates mainly as a coalition of artists concerned about the working conditions for migrant workers in the construction of museums on Saadiyat Island in Abu Dhabi, but extends beyond that.[5] The initial call for a boycott in 2011 thus emerges specifically out of a concern over worker rights and safety in just one location, but does move beyond this singular instance. Thanks to various reasons including the organizing of highly visible and mediagenic forms of conflict, the involvement of high profile artists, and the support organized through these actions galvanized largely through post-Occupy social movements networks and connections, the action was successful. Channeling the visibility generated through this outburst into a form of political antagonism that can be moved and mutates through that movement. Or as McKee describes it, Gulf Labor created a new form of artistic organizing, one that moved from the group's initial concerns to encompassing

> the inequities and complicities of the global ultra luxury economy more generally. This includes the role of art institutions in the process of gentrification, the cooperation of museums with banks and fossil fuel companies, the exploitation of the legions of precarious and low-wage workers who make the art system run, and the persistent hand-wringing on the part of artists and institutions.[6]

Arguably this dynamic where one form, or mode of conflict in the art world spills over into other issues and areas, is not confined to or unique to the dynamics of Gulf Labor. Far from it, there is a much more general dynamic of embedding layers of ethics and politics upon and in relation to one another. Thus, more than a single watermelon where the green outside contains a red and black center, today's conditions could be instead thought of as an entire watermelon patch, where a constellation of different layers and ethico-political assemblages is cultivated. As examples of this one could look at the way Liberate Tate's demand to end the role of BP's oil sponsorship at the Tate (and more broadly) overlaps with the Precarious Workers Brigade and Carrotworkers' campaigns against the art and cultural sectors' reliance on unpaid or very poorly paid labor in the form of internships.

These connections and overlaps are also quite literal in the involvement of many of the same people and their mutual support of each other (if not direct involvement). At a more conceptual level: both campaigns address a common concern about sustainability, whether in relation to ecological sustainability and climate change, or the manner in which making a living during periods of the acceptance of the hyper-exploitation of cultural work is completely unsustainable. Similarly, one could look at resonances in the conversations brought together in the 2009 Temporary Services publication *Art Work: A National Conversation About Art, Labor, & Economics* with proposals made by Gustav Metzger during the 1970s.[7] These include Metzger's famous Years Without Art, the withdrawal of labor to reshape and change the power of institutions or his demand to reduce the amount of flights taken for the continued functioning of the art world, to reduce the climate impact of the arts. Here, a point of resonance could be teased out more systematically, drawing from Brett Bloom's project *Petro-Subjectivity: De-Industrializing Our Sense of Self*[8] that looks at how oil shapes our experiences of the world. Marx once observed that men make their own history, but they do not make it as they please. Today, we could similarly conclude that while artists attempt to write their own histories, the constraining factors of labor, resources, and myriad forms of social domination are just as present, if not more than ever before.

Conceptually, links between various forms of sustainability can be made beyond using the same word to address different areas. One could turn to the work of Jason W. Moore in formulating an emergent approach to world ecology, particularly where he explores how a devaluing of key resources, or the development of what he describes as the 'four cheaps' of labor power, food, energy, and raw materials accompanies new cycles of accumulation and dispossession.[9] However, this does not mean that these resources are cheap in and of themselves. Rather, they have been made so, systematically devalued. This process of systematically devaluing a resource – whether in the form of access to the apparently infinitely abundant natural resources of colonization or the apparently free resources of unpaid domestic labor – underpins changes in the modes of production and accumulation of capital. Beneath the mystifying growth of new riches lie the supports of the same devalued, old forms of work and human activity that have been disappeared and subsumed.

We could make a similar argument about the shifts taking place within the art world. What Greg Sholette describes as its 'dark matter,' underpins the apparently magical shifts in form and approach that are – and usually in retrospect – celebrated later.[10] In other words, the condition of global cultural ecology depends on the creation of such 'cheaps' within the artistic and cultural production. While in Moore's framing the production of such 'cheaps' is mainly the outcome of conquest and colonization, in the arts and cultural world much of the dynamic of making invisible or 'darkening' of the matter of cultural labor is willfully embraced. It is what Pascal Gielen describes as the 'artistic murmuring of the multitude,'[11] or where post-Fordist work practices – characterized by highly subjective involvement yet little to not job security – were developed within the cultural sector during the 1960s, before being spreading to other sectors.[12] Initially, such practices appeared, or were presented, as a relief from the usual constraints of wage work: the formality and rigidity of the '9 to 5' workday. This 'new spirit of capitalism' first appeared as an escape from work, but such an escape was only temporary, and came at a higher cost that only became apparent later.

Re-launching Institutional Critique Today?

It was in this conjunction that institutional critique first arises, at a moment during the 1960s and 1970s where a new round of accumulation by dispossession is just being launched, where shifts in global ecology and patterns of social power are beginning to accelerate in a serious manner. Boltanski and Chiapello argue that at this very moment, the 'new spirit of capitalism' is born – born from separating the artistic and social critique, and separating politics based on the reduction of alienation from politics based on ending exploitation.[13] Or to continue with the image used to frame this chapter, the moment where the 'new spirit of capitalism' is constructed through the carving up of a watermelon – and the declaration that one can only really be concerned with either one or the other issue: either labor or the planet (or gender, or race, or any other particular 'issue'). While the history of institutional critique is usually narrated around a series of proper names, much like the post-Occupy condition that McKee describes, it would be much better understood in the context of the politics of the 1960s. While these kinds of broader movement demands and politics might be left out of art historical scholarship, it is likewise disappointing that histories of social movement politics likewise can be prone to leave out concerns that are more traditionally art world concerns, or ones that tend to stay within the art world.[14]

We can see different waves of institutional critique, where the relationship between institutional form and social movement politics shifts over time, developing. Hito Steyerl suggests that the first wave of institutional critique in the 1970s "questioned the authoritarian role of the cultural institution. It challenged the authority that had accumulated in cultural institutions within the framework of the nation state."[15] And seen within the context of the time that is quite sensible, as this was before the neoliberal turn and the process of the dismantling of such institutions really took place. Artists were confronted with cultural institutions that may have achieved some degree of autonomy from market pressures, but were nevertheless entangled into other forms of questionable power and patronage, such as through the arms trade and other problematic economic activities. These connections between boards of art institutions and the arms industry, implicating cultural institutions in the dynamics of war and oppression, initially led campaigns such as the Art Workers Coalition to call for an art strike.

The irony which Andrea Fraser points out about this, which is perhaps not surprising at all, is that this first wave of institutional critique then shifts from attempts at dismantling the institution of art towards defending the very institution that the institutionalization of the avant-garde's self-criticism had created, underpinning the potential for the very institution of critique.[16] This was in some ways a double bind: the acceptance of some forms of critique within the institutional space helped, even if in a small way, to take concerns raised about ethics, power, and representation more seriously, yet in doing so reduced the depth at which that critique operated. Or to put it another way: the institutional response would thus be to accept the grounds of critique, but to delimit them in a more circumscribed and controlled manner, so that the main issue becomes one of representation (i.e., who can appear within the institution) rather than control, power, or organization. This overlaps with the argument Steyerl makes, as she suggests that while the first wave of institutional critique produced integration into the institution, the second wave (mainly developing during the 1980s) achieved representation. From there, she adds:

now in the third phase there seems to be only integration into precarity. And in this light we can now answer the question concerning the function of the institution of critique as follows: while critical institutions are being dismantled by neoliberal institutional criticism, this produces an ambivalent subject which develops multiple strategies for dealing with its dislocation. It is on the one side being adapted to the needs of ever more precarious living conditions. On the other, the need seems never to have been greater for institutions that could cater to the new needs and desires that this constituency will create.[17]

Here Steyerl makes a number of important points, beginning with the idea that in a current third phase of institutional critique there is only integration into precarity. The critique of institutions has been weaponized against those institutions, however ambivalent, that previously might have provided some modicum of security (even if only for limited populations and in manners that were far from fair or representative). But most importantly, she gestures towards the idea of an emergent ambivalent subject, one that has to relate to institutional contexts, but does no longer believe that such spaces could provide a refuge. The institution has become a space that one might be temporarily within, but not a place that one could be of. It might be a resting place, but it cannot be a home.

A New Wave of Cooperativism?

This moves us from understanding institutions as specific spaces, or organizations, towards rethinking them as a kind of social field. We may be inside or outside the institutions, but how they operate can be continually shifting – especially as institutions, in the art world and beyond, increasingly begin to operate as networks rather than solid and fixed forms. This can be seen clearly in how artists today face equally uncertain and precarious conditions, both within and outside of institutions. What is then possible within these changing conditions? The shifting possibilities of institutional critique are not gestured towards here as an indication these histories should be discarded, but rather to indicate that as conditions change, the question is how to interact with institutions today. What would it mean to cultivate a new crop of institutional critique within and without these changing conditions?

Of course, the answers to this question are already being developed, starting from watermelon politics this chapter begins with. The strength of these emergent forms lies precisely in how they move between labor and ecology, or more generally between and around different areas, of struggle. If the new spirit of capitalism separated antagonistic demands into compartmentalized issued to be addressed, then a renewed institutional critique begins from a refusal of such separation. And so, we would suggest that the best way to create a space for maintaining such collectivity without separation would be returning to / reviving practices of cooperativism in the arts.

There is a long history of cooperatives in the arts and cultural labor, which we won't explore in depth here. The point is not to attempt to revive any particular model from this history, but rather to propose that there is much to learn from it, that would require adapting and reconfiguring for the present. Such rethinking is largely necessitated by the broad changes in the working of art institutions and the cultural economy, and the social conditions in general. Rather than returning to the question of being inside or outside the institution, the question is how to deal with constant negotiations with institutions and the shifts in the networks of how people work together and collaborate. Here we could look for examples of cooperativism in projects like the Justseeds Artists' Cooperative or the Laboratory of Insurrectionary Imagination, which have adopted such flexible model of cooperative practice and solidarity in how they organize.[18] Or perhaps we could look to the Co-op program developed by the Substation in Singapore.[19]

Platform cooperativism, as proposed by Trebor Scholz, attempts to take the best processes from the sharing economy and adapting those to creating a more just and equitable economic arrangement, rather than a platform for further corporate plunder.[20] That is to say, the precise point of platform cooperativism is not to retreat to earlier forms of cooperatives or unions, but to develop new dynamics of cooperation from within and despite the sharing economy. What would it mean to develop a form of platform cooperativism for art and cultural workers? In *Inventing the Future*, Nick Srnicek and Alex Williams make a similar argument to Scholz: a utopian left politics can be found not by retreating to past forms, but rather through a politics articulated around a series of shared and interconnected demands: embracing full automation, developing a basic income and reducing work hours, and ending the domination of work over our lives.[21] Importantly, all of these elements must come together, as a kind of 'watermelon politics,' rather than being separated into individual concerns. The separation of any one of those would just lead to yet another, new spirit of capitalism, where one form of social improvement is met by a re-articulated form of social control.

As McKee observes, today we witness a dual process where artists are withdrawing from the contemporary art system and finding ways to reinvent art as a tool of "radical imagination and direct action that in its deepest dimension asks us: how do we live?"[22] Historically, the art world and its institutions have played many roles: good, bad, and often indifferent. The question of institutional critique, of who runs the art world today (and for whose benefit) is how to occupy such spaces, even if ambivalently and briefly, but also to develop forms of cooperation and collaboration that can sustain themselves above, below, and beyond institutions, even while maintaining some relationships with them. The multiple embedded labor and ecological focus of a watermelon politics is not a solution then, but a proposal to rethink ways to cultivate such a garden of cooperative practices, and why it is more necessary than ever to do so today.

Notes

1. For more information and recent publication PDF download, see https://precariousworkersbrigade.tumblr.com/
2. For more information, see http://www.wageforwork.com/about/1/womanifesto
3. Evans, Mel (2015) *Artwash: Big Oil and the Arts.* London: Pluto Books.
4. McKee, Yates (2016) *Strike Art: Contemporary Art and the Post-Occupy Condition.* London: Verso, 7.
5. For more information on the timeline of their organizing efforts, see: http://gulflabor.org/timeline/
6. McKee, Yates (2016), 179.
7. However, you could trace this back further to the Salon de Refuses in 1863, if not before then.
8. Bloom, Brett (2015) *Petro-Subjectivity: De-Industrializing Our Sense of Self.* Ft. Wayne: Breakdown Press.
9. Moore, Jason W. (2015) *Capitalism in the Web of Life: Ecology and the Accumulation of Capital.* London: Verso.
10. Sholette, Gregory (2011) *Dark Matter: Art and Politics in the Age of Enterprise Culture.* London: Pluto Books.
11. Gielen, Pascal (2009) *The Murmuring of the Artistic Multitude: Global Art, Memory and Post-Fordism.* Amsterdam: Valiz.
12. Tokumitsu, Miya (2015) *Do What You Love: And Other Lies About Success and Happiness.* New York: Regan Arts.
13. Boltanski, Luc and Eve Chiapello (2005) *The New Spirit of Capitalism.* London: Verso.
14. Moore, Alan W. (2011) *Art Gangs: Protest and Counterculture in New York City.* Brooklyn: Autonomedia.

15 Steyerl, Hito (2009) "The Institution of Critique," *Art and Contemporary Critical Practice: Reinventing Institutional Critique*. Gerald Raunig and Gene Ray, Eds. London: MayFly Books, 14.
16 Fraser, Andrea (2005) "From the Critique of Institutions to an Institution of Critique," *Artforum* Vol. 44 Issue 1 (2005): 278-285.
17 Steyerl, Hito (2009), 19.
18 For more information on Justseeds, see http://justseeds.org. For more information on the Laboratory of Insurrectionary Imagination, see http://labofii.net.
19 For more on this, see http://www.substation.org/coop/
20 Scholz, Trebor (2016) *Platform Cooperativism. Challenging the Corporate Sharing Economy*. New York: Rosa Luxemburg Stiftung.
21 Srnicek, Nick and Alex Williams (2015) *Inventing the Future: Postcapitalism and a World Without Work*. London: Verso.
22 McKee, Yates (2016), 237.

Class Composition and the (Non) Emergence of the Multitude

> The increase of capital's domination over labor through the increasingly forced technical decomposition of tasks in order to crush politically workers' class consciousness. – Romano Alquati[1]

Around fifteen years ago, before Joanna and I started working together, I found myself spending my weekends wandering around Brick Lane in East London.[2] Living nearby in Clapton, I was fascinated not only by the space itself, but also by its social organization. Here was a former industrial area, the Truman Brewery, a sprawling nineteen-acre site, which, having been closed for its former industrial usage at some point in the 1980s, had now reopened as a weekend market for artists, cultural producers, and other 'creatives' to hawk their wares. In the place of top-down Fordist models of production and control, the space had apparently been turned over to being inhabited by networks of flexibly organized workers going about their own work and practice. At the time, I was struck to see how here was a clear example of a space that had been transformed by the transition from Fordism to post-Fordism, from a prevalence of manual and industrial labor to a hegemony of immaterial labor.

Walking around Brick Lane I thought about the declaration that Hardt and Negri made in *Empire*, namely that immaterial labor, in the expression of its own creative energies, can 'provide the potential for a kind of spontaneous and elementary communism.'[3] Excellent, I thought. Given how clearly these economic and social transformations were present in the area, then it should definitely be a hot bed of political potential, upheavals, and organizing. The networked operations of the insurgent multitude were clearly bound to reveal themselves at any second... Sooner or later... In some form... Eventually, right?

What actually transpired was nothing like the outbreak of an insurrection or the basis of anything like a spontaneous and elementary communism. Far from it. If anything, the area appeared to be filled with creative workers who were overworked, stressed, and poorly paid, but still very much highly emotionally and psychologically invested in their particular creative practice. It seemed a clear example of what CB Macpherson described as 'possessive individualism,'[4] and one where the overwhelming focus on questions of self-interest overwhelmed and blocked off discussion of collective conditions. This was interesting to me, precisely because having placed a good deal of importance on a series of concepts and arguments coming out of debates around post-autonomist thought, this was not what I had been expecting (or hoped) to find. The texts contained in this book are largely an attempt at examining why this was the case.

This led to the development, together with Joanna, of Metropolitan Factory, a workers' inquiry inspired project that was intended to tease out and understand these dynamics. In this chapter, we're not going to attempt to restate the analysis developed in that project, but rather to think through the political implications of it. In other words, debates around the changing nature of class composition and politics tended to focus around questions of immaterial and affective labor, networks, and of a multitude that would emerge from the dynamics of class recomposition.[5] These debates offered useful ideas. The problem is that their political analysis got too far ahead of the class analysis. The effects and benefits of changes in work and political composition were overstated – and what actually played out was far from the image of insurgent multitude that many of us thought would develop.

Thus, are we left in a Beckettian, absurd situation, waiting for the multitude? Perhaps. But to allude to a different Beckett piece, perhaps it's a matter of learning to fail again, and fail better. Worstward ho, comrades![6] In other words, perhaps it's less of a question about why the radical potential of the multitude was not revealed, but rather what can be made out of the event of the multitude's non-emergence. The multitude did not emerge in the expected form, yet its presence is still there – even in its apparent non-emergence. The political condition of the non-multitude is present within the dynamics of class decomposition, or how the potentials of cooperation and autonomy associated with forms of post-Fordist labor were integrated back into the operations of contemporary capitalism and social control. What this chapter will develop then is not an analysis of the multitude as concrete reality. Rather, it will attempt to further develop tools for understanding the dynamics of class decomposition, where the presence of the multitude can be registered precisely as a non-event – that, which is not present, but whose possibility constantly haunts the present.

The Future Behind Our Backs

'It's better than wages, ain't it?'
'Sure, anything's better than wages.'
– *The Misfits* (1961)

For the purposes of this chapter, we're not going to attempt to reconstruct a detailed history of the concept of the multitude, or to discuss the finer points of how the concept is used differently by key political figures. What we are mostly interested in is how the concept comes out of debates within *operaismo* and Marxist currents of the time. And somewhat more speculatively, we'd like to argue that it originates from a period where the emerging post-Fordist dynamics presented themselves as containing the potential for self-organization, but that this opening was only temporary. However, this temporary nature of the situation, before the re-imposition of the dynamics of control, or what otherwise could be theorized as class decomposition, was not taken into account in the continued usage and development of the concept of multitude. As Sergio Bologna describes it, from the point of view of these 1970s debates one could "glimpse the possibility of liberation in post-Fordism, but it was only a momentary burst."[7] It might seem, as the characters from *The Misfits* reflect upon, that anything is better than wages (i.e., long term, stable and predictable employment), but that perception passes once the reality of what follows it sinks in. It is this disjuncture between what might be described as the optimism of the concept, versus the less liberatory realities of existing conditions, that poses a problem.

There is a clear and pronounced value to retracing the concept of the multitude back to debates and developments from the 1970s. There are clear links between how the concept of the multitude has developed in the English-speaking world and what Antonio Negri theorized earlier through the concept of the "socialized worker."[8] The argument is that a new figure of labor, the socialized worker, emerges as distinct from the repetitive manual labor of the Fordist factory worker, or more generally the industrial proletariat. Production was coming to be dispersed more through productive networks rather than concentrated into specific locations, with greater value being placed on symbolic production over material assets, etc. This is the classic and well-known narrative of the transition from Fordism to post-Fordism. The most important argument brought to understanding these shifts from an *operaista* or autonomist perspective is that this transformation is not simply about the internal reorganization of capitalist labor process that has been organized and agreed upon by the goodly agents of capital itself.[9] Rather, following what, in the wake of Mario Tronti, has been referred to as a "reversal of perspective," the key point was to understand how the transformations of capitalism exist as a reactive dynamic shaped by the existing forms of working class rebellion and antagonism.

In such framing, the key task for analysis is to understand the relationship between the emerging forms of antagonism, rebellion, and political organization, and how that relates to the changing dynamics of the organization of production and sets up power relationships. This was understood and analyzed as the relationship between technical and political composition. The key conceptual development made within autonomist debates is to not fall back on the assumption that the development of capitalism is shaped by its own logic – rather, it is constantly responding to and determined by something exterior to it, namely working-class rebellion and refusal.

Thus, we would argue, if there were to be a set of concepts that autonomist thought is known for and which should be further developed today, it would not be based around the idea of the multitude, or immaterial labor. Rather, we would suggest what is far more important is the idea, or perhaps the tools, of class composition analysis itself. The virtue of class composition analysis is not to automatically understand the political possibilities of a given historical conjuncture as determined by the technical composition of machinery, the workings of management, the operations of finance and logistics, etc. That is not to claim that these have no effect, as this – to think that the changing dynamics of capital accumulation are solely shaped by class antagonism – would be perhaps to make the same mistake in the other direction. This would be to fall into another form of conceptual blindness, even if it is driven by the understandable desire to continue emphasizing the primacy of resistance.

Autonomist political theory and class composition analysis have the greatest value precisely because they attempt to analyze the constantly shifting grounds of contention between capital's attempt to re-found and reformulate the bases of its renewed accumulation, and the drive of the working class to escape from its condition that is subordinate to the demands of endless capital accumulation. This is what the tools of a nuanced class composition analysis make possible: understanding the shifts, movements, and ruptures in this ongoing tension, but without either positing or assuming either has the ultimate determining position. Althusser might tell us that in the last instance the economy is determining, but that does not necessarily need to be the case. Rather, it is a question of following out the logic of tendencies that are in operation, than assuming they will develop in any one direction.

The problem with the concept of the multitude as it has developed is not that it's wrong, per se. There is much to be said for understanding how shifts in media, technology, work, organization, and social norms are enabling and constraining forms of political possibilities within the present.[10] The difficulty is that the multitude, as a concept, emerges from within that specific moment of the emergence of post-Fordist dynamics, but before control had been re-asserted. But that was a just temporary moment, not a new condition that would be sustained. In other words, the problem is when class composition gets ahead of itself, when it mistakes a temporary condition of changing technical composition, and the politics that might be possible, for something that will continue to exist. That's not what happens. The magic moment ends, even if it does seem to re-appear with semi-regularity. Isn't the greatly celebrated freedom of the socialized workers similar to how that was claimed for the workers of the late 1990s new economy? And yet again that was claimed to be the property of the new workers of the sharing economy. The problem is, there are indeed moments of possibility that open up, that present themselves as enabling greater degrees of autonomy and self-organization. But these moments are closed off. What is needed are concepts and tools that let us understand and work through that process of closure, or what Midnight Notes describe as the "expanded new enclosures,"[11] while still holding on to the value of what enabled them. This is precisely what a focus on class decomposition enables.

Compositions

> Any division of labor within capitalist production is not only technical but also a specific mode for capital's attempts to control labor – David Camfield[12]

In *Commonwealth*, Michael Hardt and Antonio Negri provide a simple and elegant definition of class composition. They follow the long-established approach of theorizing in terms of technical composition, or "what people do at work and the skills exercised there," as distinguished from political composition, or "capacities in the field of political action."[13] The hallmark and most distinguishing feature of autonomist analysis comes down to how class composition analysis focuses on the relationship between these two different areas, ideally without making any assumptions about how one form of composition necessarily and inherently determines the other. That is to say, it is not assumed that a population is only capable of certain forms of political organizing, or is limited to forms of political organizing (they can attain trade union consciousness, but nothing more or else). At its best, autonomist analysis employs class composition to understand the shifting back and forth between forms of political and technical composition as the antagonistic actions of working subjects who develop skills and abilities that either directly or indirectly end up influencing the changing nature and shape of social and economic activity. Timothy Murphy argues that the "central methodological innovation of Italian workerism … [is] the empirical study of class composition."[14] A process of class composition then is how the social energies of working class organizing cohere into building new forms of alliance and organization. Conversely, class decomposition is the process through which capital and its agents seek to actively dissolve and break apart the forms of collectivity present within existing struggles, and, if possible, to turn them into social forms that are more beneficial to and supportive of continued, and often renewed, forms of capital accumulation and valorization.

Likewise, another central theoretical innovation can be found in the idea of the 'reversal of perspective' developed by Mario Tronti, who argued that rather than looking at the development of capital, understood as self-determining, it was necessary to understand social relations from the perspective of those attempting to rebel against and refuse the domination of capital. This had, and has, a great value, in that it reorients political analysis away from sterile structural economic analysis and places the subjectivity and collective energies of class struggle at the center of thinking as well as organizing. The difficulty is the re-orientation, while finding ways to avoid the blindness of some forms of Marxist analysis, ends up creating other forms of conceptual blindness. Not every development or change in nature of capitalism can nor should be understood as having resulted from a working-class rebellion. To think that would be to turn one form of dogmatism (such as only focusing on understanding capital itself as self-enclosed and autonomous in its development) into another, one that understands capital's development as being wholly determined by working class refusal and revolt.

This is why class decomposition is a concept that is mentioned fairly often within autonomist and post-autonomist debates, but is not developed very much as a concept in itself. To focus on it in depth sits uneasily in any framework that wants to look to the energies of class struggle as being the driving force of history. And that's understandable, but also limiting. Marx first developed the concept of decomposition in the first volume of *Capital* to understand the way in which British industrial capital developed to intensify the production and extraction of surplus value by decomposing and recomposing the ratio between living and dead labor. The notion of class decomposition, and of class composition more generally, extends this principle. Rather than trying to understand a process through which the working class is produced, it becomes a question of how class is produced over and over again. Or, perhaps, it should be described as how the working class is constituted precisely as working class repeatedly through social processes which strip away the skills, knowledge, capacities, and energies that have been developed through a process of social and political recomposition. Or, as Steve Wright suggests, the insight of autonomist thinkers, unlike many other Marxist, was understanding how

> the 'making' of the working class within a particular social formation was [not] an event confined to a single period. Rather, it was the result of an ongoing interplay between the articulations of labor-power produced by capitalist development, and labor's struggles to overcome them.[15]

The difficulty is that there is a real, and quite understandable, impetus to focus on processes of political composition, but not decomposition. Outbreaks of rebellion and class conflict are the moments of struggles and rebellions coming together. They are moments of excess when the conditions of possibility are shifted rather than just worked from within. And working from within a perspective that has been reversed, these are precisely the social processes and developments that one should be looking at.

But the very limits of this approach can be understood by returning again to the conditions of Brick Lane that this chapter began with. In many ways, the debates around immaterial labor can be understood, and should be understood, as carrying out and developing a class composition analysis. But the problem is that such an analysis can get so far ahead of itself that it loses the plot. There are a number of important things to be learned from conditions such as those. Unfortunately, the lessons available are not how different forms of immaterial labor can function as a catalyst of an elementary communism, one that could underpin the emergence of the multitude that would act in dispersed coordinated action to radically transform the world. Rather, the area was populated by creative workers displaying a high degree of possessive individualism, or a focus and drive to develop their own particular creative practice that serves to block off and prevent discussions (and organizing) focused on collective conditions.

In other words, the problem posed by Brick Lane is that changes in the shape of the technical composition of class may serve to block off and prevent the emergence of recomposition in the political sense. And given the close link between immaterial labor and at least some understandings of the multitude, it could be argued that this also prevented the formation of multitudinous social forms. In other words, these conditions could be argued to present an interesting case of class decomposition, although arguably one where the precise opposite might have been expected. Then, the question is what to do following this realization. Does this mean that all these concepts and debates can be discarded, as they clearly do not show or explain what they might have been expected to? No, not all. But it does mean they require a bit of rethinking.

Arguably, such conditions provide a good example for understanding the multitude within the present, but paradoxically not through its emergence, but rather non-emergence. In other words, the multitude can be understood not through how it concretely exists within existing workplaces, cafés, and through the metropolis, but rather through how multitudinous social forms can be approached by looking at how they are constantly decomposed within the diffuse networks of the creative economy and post-Fordist capitalism. In *Spectres of Revolt*,

Richard Gilman-Opalsky argues that systems of governance are haunted by previous revolutionary movements.[16] Arguably, new systems of labor are likewise haunted by the multitude's capacity of that which came before them. A focus on the dynamics of class decomposition could be developed to analyze these spectral presences within the operations of the contemporary economic and social order. Stanovsky productively argues that for Hardt and Negri the multitude "is the thing they see being regenerated out of the twin decompositions of class and identity politics and arising out of the new, twenty-first-century conditions of global capitalism."[17] A focus on class decomposition works from and against those processes of decomposition, first to understand them, and from there to develop new tools and practices to interrupt them and develop new avenues of social and political recomposition.

What could be developed from that perspective would be a broader and comparative analysis of the dynamic of class decomposition that are operating within the present. These could range from the operations of debt and financialization as disciplinary mechanisms,[18] to the functioning of logistical media and logistics more generally.[19] It could bring together a consideration of the rise of quantified self and surveillance of labor[20] with consideration of intensive transformations of value extraction and surplus value production in the creative industries and cultural economy[21]. A de/compositional analysis serves to highlight the ways, in which these dynamics embody the response to previous forms of class struggle, while at the same time serve to decompose those very energies. Arguably, together they function as key components of what Veronica Gago has theorized as neoliberalism from below, or

> a set of conditions that are materialized beyond the will of a government, whether legitimate or not, but that turn into the conditions under which a network of practices and skills operates, assuming calculation as its primordial subjective frame and functioning as the motor of a powerful popular economy that combines community skills of self-management and intimate know-how as a technology of mass self-entrepreneurship in the crisis.[22]

A focus on class decomposition brings together these networks of practices and skills that are operating to shape and reshape the composition of collective labor dynamics within the present. This is an important location for working through the dynamics of the multitude today, not through its presence, but how it is decomposed by the decomposing forces of the workings of neoliberalism from below. This is much different from an analysis that wants to continue on making heroic declarations about the emergence of the multitude. Steve Wright suggests that passivity on the part of the working class, broadly understood, is "easily conjured forth as a means to avoid facing the problem of class decomposition, a process every bit as real as that of recomposition."[23] But saying so is not the same as making the task of critical theory to understand the terms of defeat or paralysis. Rather, by working through processes of class decomposition, as a site of the multitude's non-emergence, it becomes possible to work through and against those conditions, perhaps even to sabotage them.

The Plural Times of the Non-Multitude

> Multitude should be understood, then, as not a being but a making – or rather a being

that is not fixed or static but constantly transformed, enriched, constituted by a process of making. This is a peculiar kind of making, though, insofar as there is no maker that stands behind the process. Through the production of subjectivity, the multitude is itself author of its perpetual becoming other, an uninterrupted process of collective self-transformation. – Michael Hardt & Antonio Negri[24]

In *Plural Temporality*, Vittorio Morfino explores how the conditions of the multitude are different because of a different relationship with time. This is the multitude's plural temporality.[25] Morfino suggests that truly understanding the radical nature of the multitude requires a "concept of temporality that is completely different from temporal coexistence."[26] For Morfino, the temporality of the multitude is to be understood instead as "the locus of the noncontemporaneous, of an impossible contemporaneity."[27] We've been suggesting in this chapter that this is what a class composition analysis, and more particularly one focused on class decomposition, affords access to. The multitude is understood not through its emergence, but through its non-emergence its ongoing decomposition. Hardt and Negri propose understanding the multitude through the ongoing process of its making. But paradoxically, if this is a process of self-transformation – of making without a maker – then it is arguably, if anything, more feasible to approach the plural times of multitude through working through and against the ongoing process of its unmaking. By understanding capital's drive to constantly decompose and unmake the multitude, which is to say working through the multitude's non-emergence, it may become possible to interrupt, sabotage, and break down these dynamics... and from there to start, yet again.

Notes

1. Quoted in Steve Wright (2003) *Storming Heaven: Class Composition and Struggle in Italian Autonomist Marxism.* London: Pluto Books, 51-52.
2. This chapter was originally drafted by Stevphen before being revised for inclusion in this book. This is the reason for the first-person pronouns used in the opening section as our attempted revisions to change that ended up sounding unnecessarily awkward. Thus, instead we have chosen this note to explain the shifts.
3. Hardt, Michael and Antonio Negri (2000) *Empire.* Cambridge: Harvard University Press, 294.
4. Macpherson, C. B. (2010) *The Political Theory of Possessive Individualism: From Hobbes to Locke.* Oxford: Oxford University Press.
5. See for instance Dowling, Emma, Rodrigo Nunes, and Ben Trott, eds. (2007) "Immaterial and Affective Labor: Explored," *ephemera: theory & politics in organization* Volume 7, no. 1.
6. Beckett, Samuel (1983) *Worstward Ho.* New York: Grove Press.
7. Bologna, Sergio (2014) "Workerism Beyond Fordism: On the Lineage of Italian Workerism." *Viewpoint.* https://www.viewpointmag.com/2014/12/15/workerism-beyond-fordism-on-the-lineage-of-italian-workerism/.
8. Negri, Antonio (1988) "Archaeology and Project. The Mass Worker and the Social Worker," in Antonio Negri, *Revolution Retrieved: Writings on Marx, Keynes, Capitalist Crisis and New Social Subjects (1967-83)* London: Red Notes, 199-228.
9. Marazzi, Christian and Sylvère Lotringer, eds. (1980) *Italy: Autonomia. Post-political politics* (New York: Semiotext(e).

10 On these overlaps see Brockman (1996), Leadbeater (2000), Pacey (2001), Campbell–Kelly (2004), Kroker, Arthur and Michael Weinstein (1994), and Huws (2003).

11 Midnight Notes (1990) *The New Enclosures*. Jamaica Plain: Midnight Notes.

12 Camfield, David (2004) "Re-Orienting Class Analysis: Working Classes as Historical Formations." *Science & Society* 68, no. 4, 438.

13 Hardt, Michael and Antonio Negri (2009) *Commonwealth*. Cambridge: Harvard University Press, 351.

14 Murphy, Timothy (2012) *Antonio Negri*. Cambridge: Polity Press, 69.

15 Wright, *Storming Heaven*, 78.

16 Gilman-Opalsky, Richard (2016) *Specters of Revolt: On the Intellect of Insurrection and Philosophy from Below*. London: Repeater.

17 Stanovsky, Derek (2009) "Organizing Marx's Multitude: A Composition on Decomposition," *Rethinking Marxism* 21, no. 2, 217.

18 Lazzarato, Maurizio (2012) *The Making of the Indebted Man*. Los Angeles: Semiotext(e). See also Martin (2002).

19 Rossiter, Ned (2016) *Software, Infrastructure, Labor: A Media Theory of Logistical Nightmares*. New York: Routledge. See also Cowen (2014).

20 Moore, Phoebe (2017) *The Quantified Self in Precarity: Work, Technology and What Counts*. London: Routledge.

21 For more on this, see Berry (2018) and Owens (2009).

22 Gago, Verónica (2017) *Neoliberalism from Below: Popular Pragmatics and Baroque Economies*. Durham: Duke University Press, 6.

23 Wright, *Storming Heaven*, 224.

24 Hardt and Negri, *Commonwealth*, 173.

25 This is not to suggest that Morfino's work is necessarily connected to a focus on class decomposition, but rather that making such a connection is potentially productive.
26 Morfino, Vittorio (2014) *Plural Temporality: Transindividuality and the Aleatory Between Spinoza and Althusser*. London: Brill, 143.
27 Ibid., 143.

Non-Conclusion: To Build Your House on the Sea

> I will not call myself an art worker but rather an art dreamer and I will participate only in total revolutions simultaneously personal and public. – Lee Lozano[1]

> Most of the work we're currently doing is dreamwork. It exists only for its own sake, or to make rich people feel good about themselves, or to make poor people feel bad about themselves. And if we simply stopped, it might be possible to make ourselves a much more reasonable set of promises: for instance, to create an "economy" that lets us actually take care of the people who are taking care of us. – David Graeber[2]

Usually conclusions are the part of the book in which ideas explored thus far are brought together in a meaningful, perhaps even dramatic, fashion. Some form of resolution is reached, which is then accompanied by teasing out some ideas to be developed in the future, or perhaps a rousing call to action. Because that isn't really the case here, it would be disingenuous to pretend otherwise, and so this section is really a non-conclusion.

The reason for this is quite simple. The central dynamic explored through this book – how the desire for meaning and fulfillment in forms of creative artistic and cultural labor ends up functioning as a disciplinary form for the cultural workers of the metropolitan factory – is not something that lends itself to an easy solution. The texts offered here were not written with the idea that there would or could be an easy solution. And even if they were, such solution would not be something that can be accomplished on the page, but only through shifts in social relationships and the organization of those labors and their context.

The driving motivation behind these texts has been something else. This book is written from a place where we've seen this dynamic as something that has affected our friends, families, and ourselves. It's not a topic chosen at random to investigate dispassionately, but something we're intimately familiar with. And even though this dynamic is by this point widespread, especially in the ever-expanding the gig economy, it's still all too common to hear people narrate it as if it is something that only affects them, as if it's some personal failing. Thus, throughout this book we have been working to fulfil a key task that C. Wright Mills attributed to the sociological imagination.[3] By this, we mean to explore and make clear the ways in which problems are often experienced as individual problems are nothing of the sort. very much embedded in the social and historical contexts they emerge from, and can only really be understood in relation to those contexts. Rather than proposing easy but useless solutions, our intent was to keep exploring these contexts and, to borrow a phrase from Donna Haraway, to stay with the trouble.[4] We have stayed with the trouble because the trouble has stayed with us, whether we wanted that or not. It's perfectly possible to feel both a deep hatred towards work in the forms of meaningless compulsion, while also not wanting the desire for alternative forms of creative labor to be rendered into a disguise for even shittier conditions.

Perhaps we should end by returning to the beginning, the book's cover. In this sense, dreamwork is our relationship to those activities, those labors, to which we return to again and again, passionately, even after being distracted and diverted by all those other things that must be done. Responsible adulting stuff. We want to stay with and affirm that desire. But the question remains – what are the necessary conditions to be able to affirm that desire?

This reminds us of something Stevphen came across years ago, back in what now feels like the Ancient Times of Live Journal.[5] It was an essay on Foucault and Deleuze that discussed dynamics similar to those explored in this book, which used the metaphor of making an attempt to build one's house upon the sea. The difficulty then is the lack of stability, the undulating motion of the waves and their moment. Or, we might see this as both a descriptive framing of the smooth spaces of overly flexible existence, or precarious conditions. With the cover star boy with the boat, we might think indeed that a boat is not a house, but arguably it is the form of living that is the most attainable upon the sea. Ultimately, the problem of precarious self-organized cultural labor is much like the question of building a boat: it's possible, but is not doable on one's own level. There may appear from time to time the mirage of such a solution, but those are not tenable for most people.

This ties in with another image-thought, namely the "Success Story" cartoon by Billy Burg, which was published in CrimethInc's *Days of War, Nights of Love*.[6] The cartoon shows a familiar scene of two women meeting up for coffee after not having seen each other for some time. They're catching up about how their lives have taken shape. But in doing so, there's an interesting gap in the conversation. The first woman, after describing her new job and career advancement, asks the other what she is doing. In response, the second woman talks about stories that she is writing. The first woman is surprised that her friend had become a writer, which is met with clarification that the other works in a restaurant. The gap here is formed around the assumption that 'what we do' collapses the question of the wage labor we perform into a proxy for our entire lives.

The second woman then describes the many things she does, from writing to sewing clothes, gardening, and playing with her new puppy... all of which are things she does, but are not 'what she does' in the context where wage labor equals identity. The point is that when we collapse 'what we do' into merely a question of wage labor, there's so much that gets left out.

Ultimately, what we're left with is not a question about art, labor, or politics in isolation, but rather nested and layered ecologies of their interactions. And ultimately, that comes back to the question of value, very much in the way that David Graeber elaborates his anthropological theory of value. Graeber's model of value is formed around understanding value as the framework for understanding the importance of our actions, as we are still enmeshed in them. Value for Graeber is not the process of public recognition of value (the "Success Story" and its embedded narratives around career success that the Billy Burg cartoon plays with and undercuts), but rather what he describes as "the way people could do almost anything (including in the right circumstances, creating entirely new sorts of social relations) assess the importance of what they do, in fact, do, as they are doing it." This is really another way of re-stating the boat problem: we must build it while we're in it, but in uncertain and changing conditions.

For this, there is not a set answer, but rather a constant experimentation that new possibilities emerge from. Perhaps these emerge even from the nightmare realities of contemporary work, as Kathi Weeks hints at when she says that while "the dream work serves to disguise the wishes that animate nighttime journeys, such wishes are revealed more clearly as the wellsprings of daydreams."[7] This book cannot tell you how to solve these various boating problems, whether passionately building them or navigating, except to say solving them likely requires putting the book down. Put the book down, talk to those around you about the conditions you're in, and what you can build together… find a way to turn those passionate drives into a force that can build new worlds – together and in common…

> it is again Spinoza who gives us perhaps the definition of true communism: passionate exploitation comes to an end when people know how to guide their common desires – and form enterprises, but communist ones – towards goals that are no longer subject

to unilateral capture; namely, when they understand that the truly good is what one must wish for others to possess at the same time as oneself. – Frédéric Lordon[8]

Notes

1. Art Workers Coalition (2008 [1969]) *AWC: Open Hearing.* April 10th, 1969. Museum of Modern Art: New York, 92.
2. Graeber, David (2021) "After the Pandemic, We Can't Go Back to Sleep," *Jacobin.* 3/4/21. https://jacobinmag.com/2021/03/david-graeber-posthumous-essay-pandemic
3. Mills, C. Wright (1999) *The Sociological Imagination.* Oxford: Oxford University Press.
4. Haraway, Donna (2016) *Staying with the Trouble: Making Kin in the Chthulucene.* Durham: Duke University Press.
5. Taylor, Joe (2005) "To Build One's House Upon the Sea." Available at https://michelfoucault.livejournal.com. This was apparently written, based upon Deleuze's dissertation, for the Turkish post-structural anarchist journal *Siyahi*.
6. Crimethinc Workers Collective (2001) *Days of War, Nights of Love: A Beginner's Guide to Crimethink.* Atlanta: CrimehInc. Free Press.
7. Weeks, Kathi (2011) *The Problem with Work: Feminism, Marxism, Antiwork Politics, and Postwork Imaginaries.* Durham: Duke University Press, 192.
8. Lordon, Frédéric (2014) *Willing Slaves of Capital: Spinoza And Marx On Desire.* London: Verso, 156.

References

Abbing, Hans (2004) *Why Are Artists Poor? The Exceptional Economy of the Arts*. Amsterdam: Amsterdam University Press.

Adorno, Theodor (1997) *Aesthetic Theory*. London: Continuum.

Alberro, Alexander and Stimson, Blake, Eds. (2009) *Institutional Critique: An Anthology of Artists' Writings*. Cambridge: MIT Press.

Antunes, Ricardo (2012) *The Meanings of Work: Essay on the Affirmation and Negation of Work*. Leiden: Brill.

Aranda, Julieta, Brian Kuan Wood, Anton Vidokle (2011) *Are You Working Too Much? Post-Fordism, Precarity, and the Labor of Art*. Berlin: Sternberg Press.

Art Workers Coalition (2008 [1969]) *AWC: Open Hearing*. April 10th, 1969. Museum of Modern Art: New York.

Arvidsson, Adam (2006) *Brands: Meaning and Value in Media Culture*. London: Routledge.

Ashley, Isaac (2012) *Bold Defiance: The Spitalfields Silkweavers: London's Luddites?* London: Past Tense.

Attali, Jacques (1985) *Noise: The Political Economy of Music*. Minneapolis: University of Minnesota Press.

Baker, Phil (2003) "Secret City: Psychogeography and the End of London," *London from Punk to Blair*. Joe Kerr & Andrew Gibson, Eds. London: Reaktion Books: 323-333.

Banks, Mark (2007) *The Politics of Cultural Work*. Basingstoke: Palgrave.

Barchiesi, Franco (2011) Precarious *Liberation: Workers, the State, and Contested Social Citizenship in Postapartheid South Africa.* Albany: SUNY Press.

Becker, Howard (2008) *Art Worlds.* Berkley: University of California Press.

Beckett, Samuel (1983) *Worstward Ho.* New York: Grove Press.

Beech, David (2016) *Art and Value: Art's Economic Exceptionalism in Classical, Neoclassical and Marxist Economics.* Leiden: Brill.

Benbow, William (n.d. [1832]). *Grand national holiday, and the congress of productive classes.* London: Pelagian.

Berardi, Franco (2009) *Precarious rhapsody: Semiocapitalism and the pathologies of the post-alpha generation.* London: Minor Compositions.

Berardi, Franco (2011) *After the Future.* Oakland: AK Press.

Berardi, Franco (2012) "The General Intellect is Looking for a Body," *Work, Work, Work: A Reader on Art and Labour.* Berlin: Sternberg Press: 89-100.

Berry, Josephine (2018) *Art and (Bare) Life: A Biopolitical Inquiry.* Berlin: Sternberg.

Bill, Frederic (2006) *The Apocalypse of Entrepreneurship.* Växjö: Växjö University Press.

Binkley, Sam (2014) *Happiness as Enterprise: An Essay on Neoliberal Life.* Albany: State University of New York Press.

Bloom, Brett (2015) *Petro-Subjectivity: De-Industrializing Our Sense of Self.* Ft. Wayne: Breakdown Press.

Böhm, Steffen and Land, Chris (2009) "No Measure for Culture? Value in the New Economy," *Capital & Class* 97: 75-98

Bohm, Steffen and Chris Land (2012) "The new "hidden abode": reflections on value and labour in the new economy," *Sociological Review* Volume 60 Number 2: 217-240.

Bologna, Sergio (2014) "Workerism Beyond Fordism: On the Lineage of Italian Workerism." *Viewpoint.* https://www.viewpointmag.com/2014/12/15/workerism-beyond-fordism-on-the-lineage-of-italian-workerism/.

Bologna, Sergio (2018) *The Rise of the European Self-employed Workforce.* Hythe: Mimesis International.

Boltanski, Luc and Chiapello, Eve (2005) *The New Spirit of Capitalism.* London: Verso.

Brougher, Kerry et al. (2010) *Yves Klein: With the Void, Full Powers.* Washington DC: Walker Art Center.

Bryan-Wilson, Julia (2009) *Art Workers: Radical Practice in the Vietnam War Era.* Berkeley: University of California Press.

Budd, John (2011) *The Thought of Work.* Ithaca: Cornell University Press.

Bunting, Madeline (2005) *Willing Slaves: How the Overwork Culture is Ruling Our Lives.* London: Harper Perennial.

Burger, Peter (1984) *Theory of the Avant-Garde.* Minneapolis: University of Minnesota Press.

Camfield, David (2004) "Re-Orienting Class Analysis: Working Classes as Historical Formations." *Science & Society* 68, no. 4: 421-446.

Campbell, Joan (1989) *Joy in Work, German Work: The National Debate, 1800-1945.* Princeton: Princeton University Press.

Campbell–Kelly, Martin (2004) *From Airline Reservations to Sonic the Hedgehog: A History of the Software Industry.* Cambridge: MIT Press.

Carlsson, Chris (2008) *Nowtopia.* Oakland: AK Press.

Casas-Cortes, Maribel and Sebastian Cobarrubias (2007) "Drifting Through the Knowledge Machine," *Constituent Imagination: Militant Investigations // Collective Theorization.* Oakland: AK Press: 112-125.

Chtcheglov, Ivan (1981 [1953]) "Formulary for a New Urbanism," *Situationist International Anthology*. Ken Knabb, Ed. Berkeley: Bureau of Public Secrets: 1-4. Available at http://www.bopsecrets.org/SI/Chtcheglov.htm.

Clammer, John (2014). *Vision and Society: Towards a Sociology and Anthropology from Art*. London: Routledge.

Colectivo Situaciones (2011) *19&20: notes on a new social protagonism*. Wivenhoe: Minor Compositions.

Countermapping Queen Mary Collective (2012) Universities in Question: Countermapping the university. *Lateral*. Available at http://lateral.culturalstudiesassociation.org.

Cowen, Deborah (2014) *The Deadly Life of Logistics*. Minneapolis: University of Minnesota Press.

Crimethinc Workers Collective (2001) *Days of War, Nights of Love: A Beginner's Guide to Crimethink*. Atlanta: CrimehInc. Free Press.

Curcio, Anna and Weeks, Kathi (2015) "Social Reproduction, Neoliberal Crisis, and the Problem with Work: A Conversation with Kathi Weeks," *Viewpoint* Issue 5. Available at https://viewpointmag.com/2015/10/31/social-reproduction-neoliberal-crisis-and-the-problem-with-work-a-conversation-with-kathi-weeks/

Dardot, Pierre, and Christian Laval (2013) *The New Way of the World: On Neoliberal Society*. London: Verso.

De Angelis, Massimo (2007) *The Beginning of History: Value Struggles and Global Capital*. London: Pluto.

De Duve, Thierry (1996) *Kant After Duchamp*. Cambridge: MIT University Press.

Dean, Jodi (2009) *Democracy and Other Neoliberal Fantasies: Communicative Capitalism and Left Politics*. Durham: Duke University Press.

Diederichsen, Diedrich (2008) *On (Surplus) Value in Art.* Berlin: Sternberg Press.

Donzelot, Jacques (1991) "Pleasure in work," *The Foucault Effect: Studies in Governmentality.* Ed. Graham Burchell, Colin Gordon, and Peter Miller. Chicago: University of Chicago Press.

Dowling, Emma, Rodrigo Nunes, and Ben Trott, eds. (2007) "Immaterial and Affective Labour: Explored." *ephemera: theory & politics in organization* 7, no. 1. http://www.ephemerajournal.org/issue/immaterial-and-affective-labour-explored

Edufactory Collective, Ed. (2009) *Toward a Global Autonomous University: Cognitive Labor, The Production of Knowledge, and Exodus from the Education Factory.* Brooklyn: Autonomedia.

Ealham, Chris (2010) *Anarchism and the City: Revolution and Counter-revolution in Barcelona, 1898–1937.* Oakland: AK Press.

Evans, Mel (2015) *Artwash: Big Oil and the Arts.* London: Pluto Books.

Federici, Silvia (2012) *Revolution at Point Zero: Housework, Reproduction, and Feminist Struggle.* Oakland: PM Press.

Federici, Silvia and Arlen Austin (2017) *The New York Wages for Housework Committee 1972-1977. History, Theory and Documents.* New York: Autonomedia.

Figiel, Joanna, Stevphen Shukaitis, and Abe Walker, Eds. (2014) "The Politics of Workers' Inquiry." *ephemera: theory and politics in organization* 14, no. 3: http://www.ephemerajournal.org/issue/politics-workers-inquiry

Findlay, Michael (2012) *The Value of Art: Money, Power, Beauty.* London: Prestel Publishing.

Fisher, Mark (2014) *Ghosts of My Life.* Winchester: Zero Books.

Fishman, William (2005) *East End 1888*. Nottingham: Five Leaves.

Fleming, Peter (2009) *Authenticity and the Cultural Politics of Work: New Forms of Informal Control*. Oxford: Oxford University Press.

Fleming, Peter (2015) *The Mythology of Work: How Capitalism Persists Despite Itself*. London: Pluto Books.

Fleming, Peter, and Carl Cederström (2012) *Dead Man Working*. Winchester: Zero Books.

Fletcher, Pamela and Anne Helmreich, Eds. (2012) *The Rise of the Modern Art Market in London, 1850-1939*. Manchester: Manchester University Press.

Florida, Richard (2005) *Cities and the Creative Class*. New York: Routledge.

Forkert, Kirsten (2013) *Artistic Lives: A Study of Creativity in Two European Cities*. Farnham: Ashgate.

Forman, Charlie (1989) *Spitalfields: A Battle for Land*. London: Hilary Shipman.

Foucault, Michel (2008) *The Birth of Biopolitics: Lectures at the Collège de France, 1978-1979*. New York: Palgrave Macmillan.

Fraser, Andrea (2005) "From the Critique of Institutions to an Institution of Critique," *Artforum* Vol. 44 Issue 1: 278-285.

Freeland, Cynthia (2001) *But Is It Art? An Introduction to Art Theory*. Oxford: Oxford University Press.

Gago, Verónica (2017) *Neoliberalism from Below: Popular Pragmatics and Baroque Economies*. Durham: Duke University Press.

Gates, Theaster (2012) *Theaster Gates: 12 Ballads for Hugenot House*. Cologne: Walther Konig.

Gauntlett, David (2011) *Making is Connecting: The Social Meaning of Creativity, from DIY and Knitting to YouTube and Web 2.0*. Cambridge: Polity.

Germer, Stefan, (2007) "Beuys, Haacke, Broodthaers," *Joseph Beuys: The Reader*. Claudia Mesch and Viola Michely. Cambridge: MIT Press: 50-65

Gielen, Pascal (2009) *The Murmuring of the Artistic Multitude: Global Art, Memory and Post-Fordism*. Amsterdam: Valiz.

Gill, Rosalind and Andy Pratt (2008) "Precarity and Cultural Work: In the Social Factory? Immaterial Labour, Precariousness and Cultural Work," *Theory, Culture & Society*, Vol. 25 (7–8): 1-30.

Gilman-Opalsky, Richard (2011) *Spectacular Capitalism: Guy Debord and the Practice of Radical Philosophy*. London: Minor Compositions.

Gilman-Opalsky, Richard (2016) *Specters of Revolt: On the Intellect of Insurrection and Philosophy from Below*. London: Repeater.

Gorz, André (2010) *The Immaterial: Knowledge, Value and Capital*. London: Seagull Books.

Graeber, David (2001) *Toward an Anthropological Theory of Value: The False Coin of Our Own Dreams*. New York: Palgrave.

Graeber, David (2021) "After the Pandemic, We Can't Go Back to Sleep," *Jacobin*. 3/4/21. https://jacobinmag.com/2021/03/david-graeber-posthumous-essay-pandemic

Graw, Isabelle (2010) *High Price: Art Between the Market and Celebrity Culture*. Berlin: Sternberg Press.

Gregg, Melissa (2011) *Work's Intimacy*. Cambridge: Polity.

Gulli, Bruno (2005) *Labor of Fire: The Ontology of Labor Between Economy and Culture*. Philadelphia: Temple University Press.

Gulli, Bruno (2010) *Earthly Plenitudes: A Study on Sovereignty and Labor*. Philadelphia: Temple University Press.

Haider, Asad, and Salar Mohandesi (2013) "Workers' Inquiry: A Genealogy." *Viewpoint Magazine*, no. 3. viewpointmag.com/2013/09/27/workers-inquiry-a-genealogy.

Hall, Stuart (2003) "New Labour's Double-Shuffle." *Soundings*, no. 24: 10–24.

Hanlon, Gerard (2015) *The Dark Side of Management: A Secret History of Management Theory*. London: Routledge.

Haraway, Donna (2016) *Staying with the Trouble: Making Kin in the Chthulucene*. Durham: Duke University Press.

Hardt, Michael and Antonio Negri (2000) *Empire*. Cambridge: Harvard University Press.

Hardt, Michael and Antonio Negri (2009) *Commonwealth*. Cambridge: Harvard University Press.

Harvey, David (2012) *Rebel Cities: From the Right to the City to the Urban Revolution*. London: Verso.

Hassan, Robert and Ronald E. Purser, Eds. (2007) *24/7: Time and Temporality in the Network Society*. Stanford: Stanford University Press.

Hern, Matt (2010) *Common Ground in a Liquid City: Essays in Defense of an Urban Future*. Oakland: AK Press.

Hesmondhalgh, David and Sarah Baker (2010) *Creative Labour: Media Work in Three Cultural Industries*. New York: Routledge.

Home, Stewart (1991) *The Neoist Manifestos/The Art Strike Papers*. Stirling: AK Press.

Hope, Sophie and Joanna Figiel (2015) "Interning and Investing: Rethinking Unpaid Work, Social Capital, and the "Human Capital Regime," *tripleC* 13(2): 361-374.

Huws, Ursula (2003) *The Making of a Cybertariat: Virtual Work in a Real World*. New York: Monthly Review Press.

Jakobsen, Jakob and Mikkel Bolt Rasmussen (Eds.) (2011) *Expect Anything Fear Nothing: The Situationist Movement in Scandinavia and Elsewhere*. Copenhagen and Brooklyn: Nebula Autonomedia.

Jones, Campbell, and André Spicer (2009) *Unmasking the Entrepreneur*. Cheltenham, UK: Edward Elgar.

Kálmán, R. and Šević, K., 2010. *We Are Not Ducks on a Pond But Ships at Sea: Independent Art Initiatives in Budapest 1989–2009*. Budapest: Impex.

Kelly, Jeff (1997) *The Best of Temp Slave*. Madison: Garnett County Press.

Klamer, Arjo (1996) *The Value of Culture: On the Relationship between Economics and Arts*. Amsterdam: Amsterdam University Press.

Knowles, Deborah (2009) "Claiming the Streets: Feminist Implications of Psychogeography as a Business Research Method," *The Electronic Journal of Business Research Methods* Volume 7 Issue 1: 47-54.

Komlosy, Andrea (2018) *Work: The Last 1,000 Years*. London: Verso.

Konings, Martijn (2015) *The Emotional Logic of Capitalism*. Stanford: Stanford University Press.

Kroker, Arthur and Michael Weinstein (1994) *Data Trash: The Theory of Virtual Class*. New York: St Martin's Press.

Robert Kurz (2016) *The Substance of Capital. The Life and Death of Capitalism*. London: Chronos Publications.

La Berge, Leigh Claire (2019) *Wages Against Artwork: Decommodified Labor and the Claims of Socially Engaged Art*. Durham: Duke University Press.

Lazzarato, Maurizio (1996) "Immaterial Labor." In *Radical Thought in Italy*, edited by Paolo Virno and Michael Hardt, 133–50. Minneapolis: University of Minnesota Press.

Lazzarato, Maurizio (2012) *The Making of the Indebted Man*. Los Angeles: Semiotext(e).

Lazzarato, Maurizio (2014) *Signs & Symbols: Capitalism and the Reproduction of Subjectivity*. Los Angeles: Semiotext(e).

Lippard, Lucy (1973) *Six Years: The Dematerialization of the Art Object*. New York: Praeger.

Lordon, Frédéric (2014) *Willing Slaves of Capital: Spinoza And Marx On Desire*. London: Verso.

Lorey, Isabell (2011) "Governmental Precarization," *Transversal* Number 8. Available at http://eipcp.net/transversal/0811/lorey/en

Lorey, Isabell (2015) *State of Insecurity: Government of the Precarious*. London: Verso.

Lucas, Rob (2010) "Dreaming in Code," *New Left Review* Number 62: 125-132.

Lucas, Rob (2010) "Sleep-Worker's Enquiry." *EndNotes*, no. 2: 154–66.

MacIntyre, Alastair (1984) *After Virtue: A Study in Moral Theory*. Notre Dame: Notre Dame University Press.

Macpherson, C. B. (2010) *The Political Theory of Possessive Individualism: From Hobbes to Locke*. Oxford: Oxford University Press.

Marazzi, Christian and Sylvère Lotringer, eds. (1980) *Italy: Autonomia. Post-political politics* (New York: Semiotext(e).

Martin, Randy (1990) *Performance as Political Act: The Embodied Self*. New York: Praeger.

Martin, Randy (2002) *Financialization of Daily Life*. Philadelphia: Temple University Press.

Marx, Karl (1880) "Workers' Inquiry." *La Revue socialiste*, April 20, 1880. Available: https://www.marxists.org/archive/marx/works/1880/04/20.htm

Marx, Karl (1976) *Capital: Volume 1*. London: Penguin Books.

Masson, Jeffrey, Ed. (1986) *The Complete Letters of Sigmund Freud to Wilhelm Fliess, 1887-1904*. Cambridge: Harvard University Press.

Mayo, Nuria Enguita (2012) "A Conversation Between Eduardo Molinari and Nuria Enguita Mayo," *Afterall* Number 30: 62-75.

McKee, Yates (2016) *Strike Art: Contemporary Art and the Post-Occupy Condition*. London: Verso

McRobbie, Angela (2002) "Clubs to Companies: Notes on the Decline of Political Culture in Speeded Up Creative Worlds," *Cultural Studies* 16, no. 4: 516–31.

McRobbie, Angela (2016) *Be Creative: Making a Living in the New Culture Industries*. Cambridge: Polity.

Merrifield, Andy (2005) *Guy Debord*. London: Reaktion Books.

Midnight Notes (1990) *The New Enclosures*. Jamaica Plain: Midnight Notes.

Mills, C. Wright (1999) *The Sociological Imagination*. Oxford: Oxford University Press.

Mitropoulos, Angela (2012) *Contract and Contagion: From Biopolitics to Oikonomia*. New York: Autonomedia.

Molesworth, Helen (2003) *Work Ethic*. University Park: Pennsylvania State University Press.

Molinari, Eduardo (2011) *The Unreal, Silver-Plated Book* San Diego: Departmento de Ficcion.

Molinari, Eduardo (2012) *Walking Archives: The Soy Children*. Wivenhoe: Minor Compositions.

Moore, Alan W. (2011) *Art Gangs: Protest and Counterculture in New York City*. Brooklyn: Autonomedia.

Moore, Jason W. (2015) *Capitalism in the Web of Life: Ecology and the Accumulation of Capital*. London: Verso.

Moore, Phoebe (2017) *The Quantified Self in Precarity: Work, Technology and What Counts*. Routledge.

Morfino, Vittorio (2014) *Plural Temporality: Transindividuality and the Aleatory Between Spinoza and Althusser*. London: Brill.

Moulier-Boutang, Yann (2012) *Cognitive Capitalism*. Chichester: Polity.

Murphy, Timothy (2012) *Antonio Negri*. Cambridge: Polity Press.

Neff, Gina (2012) *Venture Labor*. Cambridge: MIT Press.

Neff, Gina, Elizabeth Wissinger, and Sharon Zukin (2005) Entrepreneurial Labor among Cultural Producers: "Cool" Jobs in "Hot" Industries. *Social Semiotics* Volume 15 Number 3: 308-333.

Negrey, Cynthia (2012) *Work Time: Conflict, Control and Change*. Cambridge: Polity.

Negri, Antonio (1988) *Revolution Retrieved: Writings on Marx, Keynes, Capitalist Crisis and New Social Subjects (1967-83)*. London: Red Notes.

Negri, Antonio (2006) Multitude & Metropolis. http://libcom.org/library/multitude-metropolis-negri

Owens, Lynn (2009) *Cracking under pressure: The Decline of the Amsterdam Squatters' Movement*. Penn Amsterdam: Amsterdam University Press.

Pacey, Arnold (2001) *Meaning in Technology*. Cambridge: MIT Press.

Pasquinelli, Matteo (2008) *Animal Spirits: A Bestiary of the Commons*. Amsterdam: Institute of Network Cultures.

Payne, Adrian, Kaj Storbacka, and Pennie Frow (2008) "Managing the co-creation of value," *Journal of the Academy of Marketing Science* 36: 83-96.

Pink, Daniel (2010) *Drive: The Surprising Truth About What Motivates Us*. Edinburgh: Canongate.

Plan B Bureau (2009) Twenty Theses on Subversion in the Metropolis. *Occupied London*. Available at http://www.occupiedlondon.org/20theses/

Precarias a la Deriva (2006) A Very Careful Strike – Four Hypotheses. *the commoner* Number 11: 33-45.

Precarious Workers Brigade (2012) Free labour syndrome. Volunteer work or unpaid overtime in the creative and cultural sector. In E. Armano and A. Murgia (Eds.) *Mappe della precarietà vol. II: Knowledge workers, creatività, saperi e dispositivi di soggettivazione.* Bologna: I libri di Emil: 51-65.

Ranciere, Jacques (1989) *The Nights of Labor: The Workers' Dream in Nineteenth Century France.* Philadelphia: Temple University Press.

Raqs Media Collective (2009) "How to be an artist at night." In *Art school: (propositions for the 21st century.* Ed. Steven Henry Madoff. Cambridge: MIT Press: 71–81.

Rasmussen, Mikkel Bolt (2011) "To Act in Culture While Being Against All Culture: The Situationists and the Destruction of RSG-6," *Expect Anything Fear Nothing: The Situationist Movement in Scandinavia and Elsewhere.* Copenhagen and Brooklyn: Nebula / Autonomedia: 75-113

Raunig, Gerald and Gene Ray, Eds. (2009) *Art and Contemporary Critical Practice: Reinventing Institutional Critique.* London: MayFly Books.

Read, Jason (2009) "A Genealogy of Homo-Economicus: Neoliberalism and the Production of Subjectivity." *Foucault Studies* Number 6: 25–36.

Readies, DJ (2012) *Intimate Bureaucracies.* Brooklyn: Punctum Books.

Riout, Denys (2010) *Yves Klein: Expressing the Immaterial.* Paris: Editions Dilecta.

Rita, Kalmanm and Katarina Sevic (2010) *We Are Not Ducks On a Pond But Ships at Sea: Independent Art Initiatives in Budapest 1989–2009.* Budapest: Impex.

Rockhill, Gabriel (2014) *Radical History and the Politics of Art.* New York: Columbia University Press.

Roediger, David (1991) *The Wages of Whiteness: Race and the Making of the American Working Class*. London: Verso.

Roggero, Gigi (2011) *The Production of Living Knowledge: The Crisis of the University and the Transformation of Labor in Europe and North America*. Philadelphia: Temple University Press.

Ross, Andrew (2003) *No Collar: The Human Workplace and Its Hidden Costs*. New York: Basic Books.

Ross, Andrew (2009) *Nice work if you can get it: Life and labor in precarious times*. New York: New York University Press.

Rossiter, Ned (2016) *Software, Infrastructure, Labor: A Media Theory of Logistical Nightmares*. New York: Routledge.

Rossiter, Ned and Geert Lovink, Eds. (2007) *MyCreativity Reader: A Critique of Creative Industries*. Amsterdam: Institute of Network Cultures.

Rousseau, Denise (1995) *Psychological Contracts in Organizations: Understanding Written and Unwritten Agreements*. London: Sage.

Schmidt, Mary and Randy Martin, Eds. (2006) *Artistic Citizenship: A Public Voice for the Arts*. New York: Routledge.

Scholz, Trebor (2016) *Platform Cooperativism. Challenging the Corporate Sharing Economy*. New York: Rosa Luxemburg Stiftung.

Scholz, Trebor, and Laura Y. Liu (2011) *From Mobile Playgrounds to Sweatshop City*. New York: Architectural League of New York.

Scott, Allen J. (1990) *Metropolis: From the Division of Labor to Urban Form*. Berkeley: University of California Press.

Scott, Allen J. (2000) *The Cultural Economy of Cities: Essays on the Geography of the Image-Producing Industries*. London: Sage.

Scott, Allen J. (2008) *Social Economy of the Metropolis: Cognitive-Cultural Capitalism and the Global Resurgence of Cities*. Oxford: Oxford University Press.

Seidman, Michael (1990) *Workers Against Work: Labor in Paris and Barcelona during the Popular Fronts*. Berkeley: University of California Press.

Sholette, Gregory (2011) *Dark Matter: Art and Politics in the Age of Enterprise Culture*. London: Pluto Books.

Sholette, Gregory, and Oliver Ressler (2013) *It's the Political Economy, Stupid: The Global Financial Crisis in Art and Theory*. London: Pluto.

Shukaitis, Stevphen (2016) *The Composition of Movements to Come: Aesthetics & Cultural Labor After the Avant-Garde*. London: London: Rowman & Littlefield International.

Shukaitis, Stevphen, Joanna, Figiel, and Abe Walker, Eds (2014) *ephemera: theory & politics in organization* Volume 14 Number 3, issue on "The Politics of Workers' Inquiry."

Siebert, Sabina, and Fiona Wilson (2013) "All Work and No Pay: Consequences of Unpaid Work in the Creative Industries." *Work Employment Society* 27, no. 4: 711–21.

Siegelbaum, Sami (2013) "Business Casual: Flexibility in Contemporary Performance Art," *Art Journal* 72, no. 3: 48–63.

Simmel, Georg (1950) "The Metropolis and Mental Life," *The Sociology of Georg Simmel*. New York: Free Press: 409-424.

Simmel, Georg (2004) *The Philosophy of Money*. New York: Routledge.

Sinclair, Ian (1997) *Lights Out for the Territory*. London: Granta Books.

Srnicek, Nick and Alex Williams (2015) *Inventing the Future: Postcapitalism and a World Without Work*. London: Verso.

Standing, Guy (2011) *The Precariat: The New Dangerous Class*. London: Bloomsbury Academic.

Stanovsky, Derek (2009) "Organizing Marx's Multitude: A Composition on Decomposition." *Rethinking Marxism* 21, no. 2 (2009): 216-227.

Steyerl, Hito (2009) "The Institution of Critique," *Art and Contemporary Critical Practice: Reinventing Institutional Critique*. Gerald Raunig and Gene Ray, Eds. London: MayFly Books: 13-29.

Steyerl, Hito (2010) "Politics of Art: Contemporary Art and the Transition to Post-Democracy," *e-flux* # 21, December 2010. Available at http://www.e-flux.com/journal/21/67696/politics-of-art-contemporary-art-and-the-transition-to-post-democracy/

de Sutter, Laurent (2017) *Narcocapitalism: Life in the Age of Anaesthesia*. Hoboken: John Wiley & Sons.

Taylor, Joe (2005) "To Build One's House Upon the Sea." Available at https://michelfoucault.livejournal.com.

Taylor, Roger (1978) *Art, an Enemy of the People*. London: Harvester Press.

Terranova, Tiziana (2004) *Network Culture: Politics for the Information Age*. London: Pluto Press.

The Misfits (1961) Directed by John Huston, written by Arthur Miller. Seven Arts Production.

Thornton, Sarah (2008) *Seven Days in the Art World*. London: Granta.

Tokumitsu, Miya (2015) *Do What You Love: And Other Lies About Success and Happiness*. New York: Regan Arts.

Vains, Caroline (2008) "The Shopping Dérive: An embodied performance of Self in and out of time," *Drain Magazine*. Available at http://drainmag.com/ContentPSYCHOGEOGRAPHY/Essays/Vains.html

van Heur, Bas. (2010) *Creative Networks and the City: Towards a Cultural Political Economy of Aesthetic Production*. Bielefeld: Transcript Verlag.

Vishmidt, Marina (2018) *Speculation as a Mode of Production: Forms of Value Subjectivity in Art and Capital*. Leiden: Brill.

Vercellone, Carlo (2007) "From Formal Subsumption to General Intellect: Elements for a Marxist Reading of the Thesis of Cognitive Capitalism." *Historical Materialism* 15: 13–36.

Wark, McKenzie (2011) *The Beach Beneath the Streets.* London: Verso.

Warsza, Joanna, Ed. (2017) *I Can't Work Like This. A Reader on Recent Boycotts and Contemporary Art.* Berlin: Sternberg Press.

Wherry, Frederick (2012) *The Culture of Markets.* Cambridge: Polity.

Wilson, Siona (2015) *Art Labor, Sex Politics. Feminist Effects in 1970s British Art and Performance.* Minneapolis: University of Minnesota Press.

Woolfson, Charles (1982) *The Labour Theory of Culture.* London: Routledge & Keegan Paul.

Wright, Steve (2003) *Storming Heaven: Class Composition and Struggle in Italian Autonomist Marxism.* London: Pluto.

Wu, Chin-Tao (2002) *Privatising Culture: Corporate Art Intervention Since the 1980s.* London: Verso.

Zukin, Sharon (1989) *Loft Living: Culture and Capital in Urban Change.* New Brunswick: Rutgers University Press.

Zwick, Detlev, Samuel Bonsu, and Aron Darmody (2008) "Putting consumers to work. 'Co-creation' and new marketing govern-mentality," *Journal of Consumer Culture* Volume 8 Number 2: 163-196.

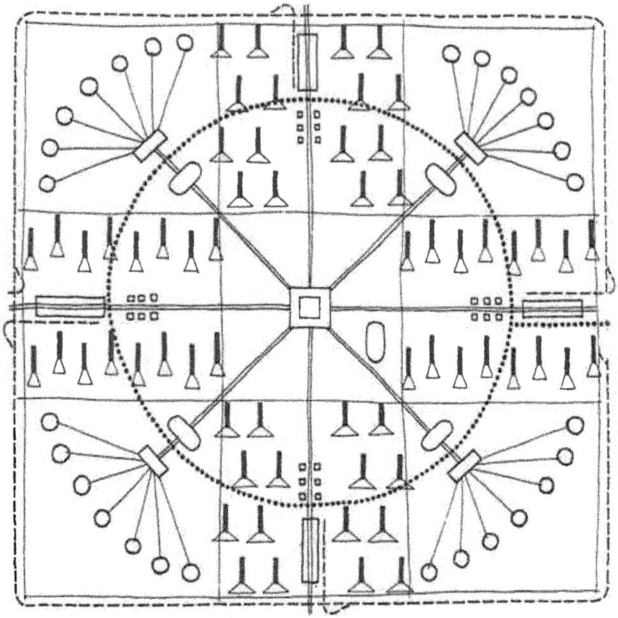

Milton Keynes UK
Ingram Content Group UK Ltd.
UKHW030609041024
449168UK00004B/78

9 781570 274077